The Dachshund

Susan M. Ewing

The Dachshund

Project Team
Editor: Dominique De Vito
Copy Editor: Carl Schutt
Design: Mary Ann Kahn
Series Design: Mada Design
Series Originator: Dominique De Vito

T.F.H. Publications
President/CEO: Glen S. Axelrod
Executive Vice President: Mark E. Johnson
Publisher: Christopher T. Reggio
Production Manager: Kathy Bontz

T.F.H. Publications, Inc.
One TFH Plaza
Third and Union Avenues
Neptune City, NJ 07753

Printed and bound in China
07 08 09   5 7 9 8 6 4
ISBN 978-079383633-8

Library of Congress Cataloging-in-Publication Data
Ewing, Susan, 1954- The dachshund / Susan Ewing.
p. cm.
Includes index.
ISBN 0-7938-3633-6 (alk. paper)
1. Dachshunds. I. Title.
SF429.D25E95 2005
636.753'8--dc22
2005009886

The Leader In Responsible Animal Care For Over 50 Years!™
www.tfh.com

///// CENTRAL
Garden & Pet

TABLE OF CONTENTS

HISTORY
OF THE DACHSHUND

The Dachshund is a popular pet in both the United States and Great Britain, and with its two versatile sizes and three coat types, that's no surprise. Add their happy attitude and their determination and you've also got a versatile dog for showing, performance events, and hunting. How did we get this wonderful breed?

For those willing to go way back, evidence suggests that dogs began their association with man between 10,000 and 14,000 years ago. Dog historians seem to agree that *Canis lupus*, the wolf, in one form or another, is the ancestor of all the breeds of *Canis familiaris*, the dog, in all the many forms that it takes today. This is pretty amazing when you consider the American Kennel Club recognizes over 160 breeds and varieties in seven Groups—Sporting, Hound, Terrier, Non-Sporting, Toy, Working, and Herding—with dogs ranging in size from Chihuahuas to Irish Wolfhounds. There are many more unrecognized breeds around the world.

EARLY DACHSHUNDS

For decades, the Germans bred Dachshunds in three sizes: Teckel, Miniature Teckel, and Rabbit Teckel, rather than just the two sizes—standard and miniature—found in Great Britain and the United States.

The first organized dog show in England was held in 1859, but only Pointers and Setters were entered. By 1870, participants in showing felt that a controlling body was necessary to set basic rules regarding dog shows. In April of 1873, 12 men met in London and founded the Kennel Club.

Although the Kennel Club marks its beginning as 1873, registration records only go back as far as 1908, at which time hundreds of Dachshunds were registered, so there's no way to know the name of the first registered Dachshund. The Dachshund Club was founded in 1881, so the dogs were obviously very popular before the Kennel Club accepted them. In 1927, the Wirehaired Dachshund Club was formed, and in 1929, the Longhaired Dachshund Club was formed.

World Wars I and II saw a huge decline in both the popularity and population of Dachshunds in both the United States and Great Britain because of their association with

Germany. With the perseverance of dedicated breeders on both sides of the Atlantic, as well as the winning qualities of the dogs themselves, the Dachshund's numbers rebounded quickly, perpetuating the breed.

THE VON MARIENLUST LEGACY

One of the leading Dachshund kennels in the 1930s was owned by Josef and Maria Mehrer of West Hempstead, New York. Their kennel name was von Marienlust. According to Anne Gordon in *The Dachshund: A Dog for Town and Country*, the founding of the von Marienlust kennel was, "a defining moment in the development of the Dachshund in the twentieth century." This kennel, and other serious breeders of the time, worked to produce a dog lower on leg with a deeper chest, straighter legs and feet, and a level topline.

The best known of the von Marienlust dogs was Ch. Favorite von Marienlust, who helped to set the type for the modern Dachshund. He sired over 100 champions and set his stamp on them. Bred by the Mehrers, he was owned by Fred and Rose Heying of Heying-Teckel Kennels in California. The Heyings bred Ch. Falcon of Heying-Teckel, whose father was Favorite. Falcon sired around 80 champions himself.

In Longhairs, Bayard Kennel, owned by Mary Howell, was a strong influence, producing beautiful heads, correct fronts, and good ribbing.

Many present-day Wirehairs owe their correct harsh coat and substance to Ch. Vantebe's Draht Timothy, bred by Betty W. Dukes and owned by Peggy Westphal of von Westphalen Kennel, and Ch. Pondwick's Hobgoblin, imported from England by Nancy Onthank of Rose Farm Kennel.

HOLDING THE LINES

Today's breeders are just as devoted to the little dog and are working hard to maintain breed type and temperament.

The Dachshund, or Teckel, as he is called in Germany, has been known since the Middle Ages and is thought to have evolved from dwarf mutations of taller hunting hounds, possibly the Schweisshund or the Bibarhund, with possible crosses with terriers and/or spaniels to obtain the wire and long coats.

Laddland Kennels has produced quality Smooth Dachshunds for years, and Ch. Laddland A Wing and A Prayer holds the record as top producer with over a hundred champions to his credit. In Longhairs, Walmar Kennel has had a great influence.

In Wirehairs, top kennels include Judy Anderson's Schoolhouse Kennel, Fred and Carol Vogel's Brodny Kennel, and Liz Heywood's Starbarrack Kennel. In 1997, Ch. Starbarrack Malachite was a top-winning Wirehair who won the Hound Group at Westminster, which was quite an accomplishment.

While dedicated breeders large and small are mainly responsible for maintaining the integrity of any breed, clubs also play a role in breed continuity.

How Registries Support Breeders

Both the American Kennel Club and the Kennel Club in Britain support purebred dogs by serving as a registry for dogs and setting rules and regulations for competitive events, which in turn serve as a showcase for each particular breed, as is evidenced by this quote from the Kennel Club: "The basis of breed shows is the judging of dogs against the 'Breed Standard', which is the prescribed blueprint of the particular breed of dog. For all licensed breed shows, the Kennel Club Breed Standards must be used for the judging of dogs. The Kennel Club owns the Breed Standards, and all changes are subject to approval by the Kennel Club General Committee. New Breed Standards, for newly recognized breeds, are drawn up once the breed has become sufficiently established within the UK. Careful research is conducted into the historical background, health, and temperament of any new breed before Kennel Club recognition is granted."

The Ever-Popular Dachshund

The Dachshund has been among the top ten most popular dogs based on registration with the American Kennel Club for decades. In the United Kingdom, the Kennel Club breaks down Dachshund registrations by both size and coat type. In 2003, the miniature Longhaired Dachshund was 31st in popularity; the Smooth-coated mini was 37th; and the Wirehaired mini was 57th. The Wirehaired standard held 84th place; the Longhaired standard came in 102nd; and the Smooth-coated standard Dachshund was in 104th place.

Today's Dachshund breeders understand the importance of breed type and temperament, just as did early devotees of the Dachshund.

The AKC mission statement says that the American Kennel Club will "maintain a registry for purebred dogs and preserve its integrity, sanction dog events that promote interest in, and sustain the process of, breeding for type and function of purebred dogs. Take whatever actions necessary to protect and assure the continuation of the sport of purebred dogs."

THE DACHSHUND CLUB OF AMERICA

National breed clubs focus on a specific breed and work to encourage proper breeding programs. Some national breed clubs are formed before a breed is accepted by the AKC as a way to maintain official breeding records. Some clubs are formed after a breed is accepted. The Dachshund Club of America was founded in 1895. All national breed clubs write the breed's official standard. Most breed clubs offer special awards to champions in their breed, as well as such awards as Register of Merit to bitches and dogs who have produced or sired a specific number of champions. Breed clubs may also offer awards to dogs who earn titles in three or more areas of AKC competition, such as conformation, obedience, and agility.

Breed clubs frequently offer guidelines to their members,

The AKC organizes breeds into seven Groups: Sporting, Hound, Working, Terrier, Toy, Non-Sporting, and Herding. The Dachshund is a member of the distinguished Hound Group.

encouraging ethical behavior in both breeding and selling puppies. While there is no way that a club can enforce their standards, other than refusing membership, most members of most breed clubs do respect these principles. Here is the code of ethics of the Dachshund Club of America, and their membership guidelines.

National breed clubs encourage proper breeding through guidelines and special programs for its members. This helps Dachshund breeders—and owners—understand and value the Dachshund.

The DCA Code of Ethics

"This code is set forth with the realization that ethics cannot be legislated and that most individuals intend to do what is right. The purpose of the code is to set forth principles of practice that the DCA Board would like to have its members adhere to as they strive to preserve the quality of the breed. The code represents the minimum in ethical practices, not rules or laws, and carries no sanctions other than the dictates of one's conscience as he or she strives to promote and protect Dachshunds."

DCA Membership Guidelines

The objects of the Dachshund Club of America are to encourage and promote quality in the purebred breeding of the Dachshund and to do everything possible to bring their natural qualities to perfection; to encourage the organization of independent local Dachshund Specialty Clubs in those localities where there are sufficient fanciers of the breed to meet the requirements of the American Kennel Club; to urge members and breeders to accept the standard of the breed as defined by the Dachshund Club of America and approved by the American Kennel Club as the only standard of excellence by which Dachshunds shall be judged; to do all in its power to protect and advance the interests of the breed and to encourage sportsmanlike competition at dog shows, field trials, obedience trials, and earth dog tests; to conduct sanctioned matches and specialty shows, field trials, obedience trials, and earth dog tests under the rules of the American Kennel Club.

Membership is open to *serious fanciers* who have demonstrated a significant on-going interest in the Dachshund, who are in good standing with the American Kennel Club, subscribe to the objects of the Dachshund Club of America, and agree to abide by the By-laws of the Dachshund Club of America, its Code of Ethics, and the rules of the American Kennel Club. For more information, go to the AKC's website at www.akc.org.

Fanciers participate in dog shows around the country and around the world that are sanctioned by organizations like the American Kennel Club in the US or the Kennel Club in the UK.

THE AMERICAN KENNEL CLUB

The AKC was founded in 1884, and in 1886 it was decided that a reliable record of pedigrees was an important part of the sport of purebred dogs. At the time there were two existing studbooks, the American Kennel Register and the National American Kennel Club. The National American Kennel Club gave its studbook to the American Kennel Register. These books, which contained 5,397 dogs, became the basis of the American Kennel Club Studbook, which is continued to this day. The AKC has offices in New York and in Raleigh, North Carolina, and is managed by a 12-member Board of Directors. The AKC is made up of over 500 dog clubs. Sometimes called the "Club of Clubs," there are also almost 4,000 affiliated clubs. A delegate represents each member club. The delegates elect the Board of Directors.

In addition to setting the rules for dog shows and a variety of performance events, the AKC maintains a library in New York, a Museum of the Dog in St. Louis, and in 1994, formed the AKC Canine Health Foundation, which raises and distributes money for canine health research. The AKC also offers scholarships for veterinary students. The AKC maintains a national database service for Companion Animal Recovery, which records permanent identification, such as tattoos and microchips.

As a registry organization, the AKC registers both litters and individual dogs. When a breeder registers a litter, the AKC sends that person a blue slip for each puppy. This blue slip should be given to the puppy buyer at the time of purchase; the owner then sends that slip to the AKC, along with a registration fee. There are two types of registration, full and limited. A full registration means that that dog's offspring may be registered with the AKC. A limited registration means that any offspring are unregisterable. The breeder, and only the breeder, may change the designation from limited to full at any time.

The reason for the limited registration is that if, in the breeder's opinion, the dog sold does not conform to the breed standard, or if the dog has been sold as a pet for any reason, the limited registration prevents a fault from being passed on. Usually, the buyer must agree to neuter the dog, but in case he or she does not, the limited registration prevents them from registering any puppies.

Applying to the DCA

If you feel you want to become more involved in breeding and showing dogs, or membership in the Dachshund Club of America appeals to you for other reasons, you can contact them through the address listed in the Resources section of this book. They will be happy to provide additional information. You can also look for the web site of the DCA online.

CHARACTERISTICS
O F   T H E   D A C H S H U N D

There's no mistaking the Dachshund. The breed comes in two sizes (standard and miniature) and three varieties (Smooth, Longhaired, and Wirehaired.) Both sizes and all three varieties are judged by the same "standard," which includes references to the three coat types. While the breed standard describes the weight of the standard-sized Dachshund as between 15 and 32 pounds, most show dogs are between 18 and 22 pounds. Miniatures are less than 11 pounds. Some Dachshunds fall in between and are called "tweenies" by fanciers.

No matter what size or variety, this long-in-body and short-of-leg dog is a bold, confident, intelligent, and alert companion. Dachshunds were bred for hunting, for flushing out game, and if necessary, for following his quarry into a den or burrow. He has a good nose and a loud bark, making him ideal for trailing and for letting the hunter know just where he is.

HOW A STANDARD DEFINES A BREED

A standard is a written description of a purebred dog. It's like a blueprint for breeders, telling them what "perfection" is in any given breed. No dog is perfect, of course, but all responsible breeders do so with an eye to the standard of perfection, trying to make each generation of dog better than the one before.

The American Kennel Club approves the standard of each breed it registers, but the parent club is responsible for writing that standard. Each AKC recognized breed has a national, or "parent" club that writes the original standard and any revisions that may follow as the years go by.

If you read the standard of a purebred dog, you will have a good idea of what the dog should be like, even if you've never met that particular breed. The standard will describe the build of the dog, starting with the head. Should the dog's ears stand straight up, or hang down? How long or short is the nose? Is there a preferred shape of eye? You'll find the answers in the standard. The complete official standard for the Dachshund is in the Appendix.

The Standard as a Blueprint for the Breed

The standard will tell you what the correct proportions of a specific dog should be. Corgis and Dachshunds are longer than they are tall. Pugs should be square. Many standards will

Dachshunds come in two sizes (standard and miniature) and three varieties (Smooth, Longhaired, and Wirehaired). This photo shows a Smooth with a Longhaired Dachshund.

make reference to the purpose for which a dog was bred. If you want a dog to pull a sled for miles at a time, you want a dog with strength and a good coat. Although Dachshunds have strength, a smooth coat would not survive in the frozen north, and those short legs wouldn't cover much ground.

The Dachshund was developed as a hunting dog, and the standard reflects that. There is an emphasis on a strong jaw with full dentition. The chest must allow enough room for the lungs to retain oxygen when the dog is working underground. No matter what his coat type, a Dachshund should still have the instinct to hunt, as well as the nose and voice that goes with that instinct. A Dachshund is built to go into burrows. Those short, strong legs help to push the dog into the tunnel, and the keel-like breastbone also helps as he goes after his prey.

The Dachshund Standard

If you're reading this book to see if a Dachshund is right for you, read the entire standard in the appendix. If you've already chosen your Dachshund, read the standard anyway and see how close your dog comes to the ideal. Remember, though, that no dog is perfect, and if you're not planning to breed or show your dog, a fault doesn't matter if it doesn't threaten the dog's health. So what if your pet is a little long in the leg or has a less-than-perfect tail? Enjoy his wonderful personality, and be thankful every day that you have a Dachshund.

A standard will also describe the temperament of the breed, and this is perhaps the most important information of all. Dachshunds may be small, but they were bred to hunt badger, which means they are not timid. They will stand up for themselves, even if that means not backing down from a larger dog. They can be fearless and may try to be a bit bossy. Says the AKC standard, the Dachshund is "clever, lively, and courageous to the point of rashness, persevering in above and below ground work."

The Dachshund was developed as a hunting dog, and his entire structure supports that purpose, from his strong jaws to his short legs.

Making Changes to the Standard

The Dachshund Club of America is in the process of considering changes to the AKC breed standard regarding piebalds and double dapples. A revision is not something that is easy to do. A committee generally works on whatever revision may be suggested, and then the revised standard is voted on by the club membership. Rules vary within each club, but frequently, standard revisions need to be approved by two-thirds of the membership.

In the United Kingdom, the system is a bit different. There, the Kennel Club owns the Breed Standards and all changes are subject to approval by the Kennel Club General Committee. Breed Standards for newly recognized breeds are drawn up once the breed has become sufficiently established within the UK. The background of the breed, as well as health and temperament, is researched before Kennel Club recognition is granted.

The Dachshund is the only AKC-recognized breed that hunts both below and above the ground.

A Dachshund has a black nose, tight lips that cover a strong jaw, a slight stop between the muzzle and skull, and dark-rimmed, almond-shaped eyes.

THE DACHSHUND'S PHYSICAL FEATURES

Everyone knows the basic "long and low" shape of the Dachshund, but there's more to the Dachshund than that. Let's start at the tip of the nose, which should be black. Then, let's travel back over the tight lips, where there is no drooling with a Dachshund. Those lips cover a strong jaw, with equally strong teeth. Remember, the Dachshund is a hunting dog and needs to be able to deal with whatever prey he is after. Those teeth meet in a scissors bite, and anything other than a scissors bite is a fault. The muzzle is slightly arched, and there's very little stop between the muzzle and the skull.

Next come the eyes, dark rimmed and almond shaped. The eyes are very dark and should have an "energetic, pleasant expression." The Dachshund's ears are set near the top of his head and are medium length and rounded. When the dog is animated, the forward edge of the ear just touches the cheeks so that the ears frame the face.

Now, follow the slightly arched neck down to the Dachshund's shoulders. The long Dachshund back runs in a straight line from the withers, and the abdomen is slightly drawn up. The Dachshund may be short, but he's not droopy. His skin is loose to prevent tearing as he tunnels into a burrow.

The Dachshund's ribs are well sprung and oval, allowing plenty of room for heart and lungs, and the breastbone is

The Dachshund may be short, but he's not droopy; the standard calls for a long back, a slightly drawn-up abdomen, and well-muscled hindquarters.

prominent in front. Long, broad shoulder blades, an upper arm at a right angle to the shoulder blades, and short forearms, all covered with strong muscle, make him an ideal digging machine. The joints between the forearms and the feet are closer together than the shoulder joints, so the front does not appear absolutely straight. The paws are full, tight, and compact, with well-arched toes and tough, thick pads. They may be equally inclined slightly outward. Front dewclaws (the fifth toe above the heel) are usually removed.

The Dachshund's hindquarters are also strong and well muscled. All the joints form a series of right angles, and from the rear, the thighs look strong and powerful. When viewed from behind, the back legs are upright and parallel. The hind paws are a bit smaller than the front paws, again with arched toes and tough pads. The hind foot points straight ahead. Rear dewclaws should be removed.

The tail is a continuation of the spine and should have no kinks, twists, or curves. Long ago, hunters used that long, strong tail as a handle, a way to grab onto and haul the Dachshund out of a burrow or den.

The Dachshund in Motion

When talking about movement in a Dachshund, it's a good idea to remember that they were bred as hunting dogs. Movement should be smooth and the forelegs should reach well forward, without much lift, in unison with the driving action of the hind legs. There's no wasted energy in this kind of movement, and dogs who are out in the field trailing game need to conserve energy. The legs do not move in exact parallel planes but incline slightly inward to compensate for shortness of leg and width of chest.

Hind legs drive on a line with the forelegs, with hocks straight. If the dog is moving correctly, the rear pads should be clearly exposed during rear extension. Feet must not swing out, cross over, or interfere with each other. Short, choppy movement or a rolling or high-stepping gait are both wrong. The working Dachshund needed agility, freedom of movement, and endurance to do his job, and breeders still strive for those ideals today.

Colors

When it comes to color, Dachshunds have quite a variety. Many Dachshunds are red, ranging from a light red, which may appear reddish blond, to a rich, deep shade of red similar to that of an Irish Setter, with or without a shading of interspersed dark hairs. Cream is also an accepted color, though rarely seen. A small amount of white on the chest is acceptable but not desirable.

Two-colored Dachshunds include black, chocolate, wild

Red, black, and tan are common Dachshund colors.

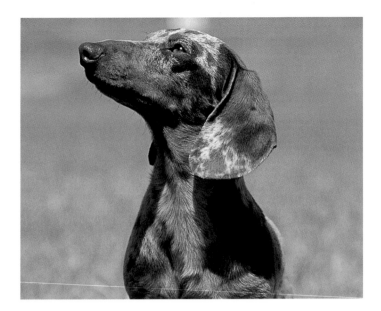

Dachshunds also come in piebald and dapple color patterns.

boar, gray (blue), and fawn (Isabella), each with tan markings over the eyes, on the sides of the jaw and underlip, on the inner edge of the ear, front, breast, inside and behind the front legs, on the paws and around the anus, and from there to about one-third to one-half the length of the tail on the underside. Wild boar is a combination of light and dark hairs that give the dog a salt-and-pepper appearance. Again, there may be a small amount of white on the chest.

There are also dappled Dachshunds. The "single" dapple pattern has lighter-colored areas contrasting with a darker base color. Both colors should be equal in area. A larger patch of white on the chest of a dapple is allowed. A "double" dapple is one in which varying amounts of white coloring occur over the body in addition to the dapple pattern.

Piebald is not a recognized color pattern in the Dachshund standard, although it is listed on the AKC registration forms and has become popular with pet buyers. The piebald gene is recessive and doubles the white gene, which can result in eye and ear problems. If this is the color you want or already have, ask the breeder about any health issues that exist or may come up. Double dapple can also result in serious health issues, resulting in small eyes, no eyes, or hearing issues.

Brindle is a pattern (as opposed to a color) present in some Dachshunds in which black or dark stripes occur over the entire body, although in some specimens the pattern may be visible only in the tan points.

Coat Types

Now, let's look at the three coat types. A Smooth Dachshund has a smooth, close coat, which shouldn't be very thick, although long bristles may show up on the dog's underside. However, this is not a fault. The tail should be covered with hair, but it shouldn't have any hint of fringe.

In Wirehaired Dachshunds, with the exception of the jaw, eyebrows, and ears, the whole body is covered with a uniformly thick, rough, hard outercoat and a finer, somewhat softer, shorter undercoat distributed between the coarser hairs. The absence of an undercoat is a fault. Wirehaired Dachshunds have a beard and eyebrows. On the ears, the hair is shorter than on the body and is almost smooth. There should be no soft outercoat anywhere on a wirehaired Dachshund, and no long, curly, or wavy hair. The tail should have lots of hair and should gradually taper to a point. The most common colors in a Wirehair are wild boar, black and tan, and shades of red, but all colors are allowed.

If you have a Longhaired Dachshund, you have a dog with a sleek coat of longer hair. Frequently, longer, slightly wavy hair is found under the neck, on the chest, on the ears,

The Longhaired Dachshund has sleek, longer hair; the Smooth has a short, close coat; and the Wire has a thick, rough outercoat and finer undercoat as well as a defined beard and eyebrows.

behind the legs, and on the underside of the body. Too profuse a coat, equally long hair over the whole body, a curly coat, or a pronounced parting on the back are faults. As for the tail, the hair is longest there.

ARE YOU READY FOR A DACHSHUND?

Take the time to find out all you can about Dachshunds before you make a commitment that could last 14 to 16 years or more. Talk to breeders and owners. Ask a veterinarian questions. If possible, go to a dog show, watch Dachshunds in the ring, and talk to handlers. Try to do all of this before you actually get a Dachshund puppy.

Presumably, if you're at the stage where a puppy is crawling into your lap, you've done some homework and are seriously looking for an addition to your family. If you aren't already looking, take a minute to think about what having a puppy means. Do all the members of the family want a dog? If there are children, their vote is probably yes. They may even say they will take care of the dog. They may even mean it, but depending on their age, they may not be able to do everything for the dog. They might eventually ignore the unpleasant aspects of dog care and may lose interest after the novelty has worn off. It's up to the adults in a family to commit to the care of the dog for his lifetime. In the case of a Dachshund, that is usually 14 to 16 years. If the person

Although there are slight differences in temperament among the varieties, and even from dog to dog, generally speaking the Dachshund is a lively dog who is "courageous to the point of rashness." This can get him in trouble, as he will not hesitate to confront dogs much larger than he is, but it also makes him a wonderful watchdog.

Learn as much as you can about all aspects of the Dachshund before deciding if it's really the breed for you.

Who wouldn't find these puppies irresistible? Their charm doesn't make them the right breed for everyone, however.

who will be the primary caregiver doesn't really want a dog, then a dog is not a good idea. If the adults in the family want a dog and are willing to take care of that dog's needs, from food and water to housetraining to necessary visits to the veterinarian, not to mention playtime and exercise, then it's time to choose the right Dachshund for your family.

Grooming Requirements

For starters, there's the question of coat. If you get a Dachshund, you will be getting hair in varying degrees. Even the smooth Dachshunds shed. The hairs are short and work their way into carpets and upholstery. Longhaired Dachshunds will require more grooming to keep mats from forming, and the Wirehaired variety will also require grooming to keep them looking neat and tidy. Think about how much time you want to spend grooming or if you want to consider regular trips to your local groomer.

Temperament

The official standard for the Dachshund describes the breed as having a "hunting spirit" and "persevering in above and below ground work, with all the senses well developed." This is why a fenced yard is so important. If a Dachshund picks up the scent of a rabbit or squirrel, he's going to follow that scent, and he's not going to be paying attention to oncoming traffic if that trail should happen to cross a road.

Your Dachshund and Training

The character of the Dachshund has been described as intelligent, happy, disobedient, self willed, and affectionate. The intelligent, disobedient, and self-willed parts of your Dachshund mean you should definitely consider some obedience training, even informally, or your Dachshund will soon be trying to run the household. You may never want to compete in formal obedience trials, but it's always a good idea to teach your Dachshund some basic commands. While you can learn how to do this in Chapter 6 of this book, a good class will also help you to socialize your Dachshund, getting him used to other people and dogs.

Dachshunds aren't usually afraid of bigger dogs, either, even when they should be. It's fine for your Dachshund to play with other dogs, but make the introductions gradually, making sure everyone wants to play and is friendly. If the dog is much bigger than your Dachshund, be cautious. A large dog can accidentally harm a smaller one.

Like all dogs, Dachshunds know how to get what they want, and they're so cute that it's hard not to give in. But don't let that cute little puppy sleep at the foot of the bed or curl up on the couch next to you if you won't want the adult doing the same thing. If you intend to let your adult sleep with you, fine, but if not, don't start.

While Dachshunds are hunting dogs and happy to follow a trail, they are also very much "people" dogs. They need to be a part of the family, not shut away in their crates or left out in the yard.

Low, but All Go

Dachshunds are short, but they have a bold nature, and they won't hesitate to launch themselves from your bed or the couch or even a grooming table. If, for whatever reason, they are up on a relatively high surface, help them to the ground. Constantly jumping down from high places can lead to back and shoulder injuries. If you enjoy having your Dachshund with you on a high bed or couch, consider building or buying a doggy ramp.

Physically, Dachshunds are short and don't weigh much. This means that you can pick them up if you have to, which can be an advantage when your dog is sick and can't jump into the car on his own for that trip to the veterinarian's office. They are sturdy enough, though, to play with children and not get injured if the play should get a little rough, although children should be taught to always be gentle with the dog.

Their small size makes it convenient to pick Dachshunds up and carry them. Help them up and down from high places so they don't injure their backs.

Exercise Requirements

Your Dachshund will need some daily exercise, of course, but definitely not as much as a larger dog. Indoor games can give your Dachshund some exercise, and a brisk walk around the block a couple of times a day should do just fine. If jogging is your favorite activity, though, you should know that Dachshunds are not built for long runs. While they certainly can (and do) cover ground when hunting, running is not their best trait.

If you have a Smooth coat, consider a doggy sweater in

Dachshunds need daily exercise; in a fenced yard or enclosed area, a run off-leash is a joy for your dog.

the winter months when your Dachshund is outdoors exercising. If you have a fenced yard, never leave your Dachshund unattended for long. In the summer months, make sure there's shade and plenty of water available. If you don't have a fenced yard, keep your Dachshund on a leash; a loose Dachshund is a lost Dachshund.

Dachshunds are more than willing to cuddle on the couch, but they're even more willing to be active. Some Dachshunds will retrieve toys for as long as you'll throw them. Some will entertain themselves in the yard chasing squirrels, and some want a nice, brisk walk to check out all the sights and sounds of the neighborhood. Whatever they do, Dachshunds like to do it with their people!

Eating Requirements

Dachshunds are chowhounds. They love to eat and can look quite pathetic when you're having a snack and they're not. The amount of food a Dachshund will need will depend on how active he is, so you may need to do a bit of adjusting before you discover the right amount of food. A miniature may only need half a cup a day, while a standard may need a cup. (More on feeding in Chapter 4.)

Once you determine the right amount for your dog, try to stick with that amount. Overweight animals can suffer poor health, just like overweight humans. They can develop joint problems, heart disease, and diabetes. The occasional

A Dachshund's needs and personal characteristics will determine his suitability to your lifestyle.

Singing the Dachshund's Praises

Murray Weinstock was inspired by his dog Sparky to write "The Dachs Song," and Paul de Vries put music to the lyrics.

There's no other dog like a dachshund,
Walking so close to the ground.
They're stubborn and sly as a fox and
The happiest pet to be found.
Most kind of dogs seem to either
Have shapes or proportions all wrong;
They're only one way or the other,
But Dachshunds are both short and long.
Chorus:
Dachsie, meine dachsie,
The best canine under the sun,
Call you "wiener" or "sausage" or "hot dog"
We know that you're number one.
© 1992 Furry Murray Music

bit of cheese or leftover scrambled egg won't kill your Dachshund, but don't overdo it, and unless you want to turn your lovable Dachshund into an annoying pest, don't ever feed him from the table.

Watchdog

If you're looking for a watchdog, the Dachshund may be the perfect choice. A Dachshund will definitely let you know if someone knocks on your door, and they'll keep letting you know until you do something about it.

Sociability
With Pets

If you have other pets, make introductions gradually and your new dog will fit right in. Dachshunds and cats *can* be friends, especially if introductions are made when your Dachshund is a pup. If your Dachshund is an adult and you're bringing home a kitten, control all meetings between dog and cat, and make the introductions gradual. You might want to start with the cat in a room with a closed door and let the animals sniff each other through the crack. With the first face-to-face meeting, keep the dog on a lead and always make sure that the cat has an escape route or a high shelf for safety.

If you already have a dog, be cautious when introducing

As with any breed, socialization when the dog is young is an important part of his development. Any dog can be fearful, shy, or aggressive. It's up to you to introduce your Dachshund to new people and places in a way that makes it all a positive experience and helps your Dachshund grow up to be a welcome addition to the family.

your new Dachshund. Choose a neutral place for the first meeting. Keep both dogs on lead, but try to keep the leads loose. A tight lead can tell the dog there is something to fear and can lead to aggression. Think about the temperament of the current dog. Talk to the breeder or others who may have a Dachshund in a multi-dog household. Generally, if the other dog is friendly, the Dachshund will be just fine.

Although two males may not get along, your Dachshund should be able to live with other pets in the household. Whether it's another Dachshund or some other breed, if the dogs are introduced properly, you shouldn't have a problem. While an individual Dachshund may get along with individual guinea pigs, birds, hamsters, or even mice, remember that with all of these animals, they would be prey for the dog predator in the wild. This is why it's important never to leave any dog with any small pet unless you are closely supervising.

Dog toys appeal to dogs because the toys make a high-pitched squeaky sound. Small, furry animals make a very similar sound. Keep those other pets safe, even if your Dachshund seems inclined to be friendly. Remember that your Dachshund was bred to be a hunter.

With Children

Most children will ask for a dog at some point, and most parents, if it's possible, will want to get their child a dog. Getting a family dog can be a wonderful experience, but remember, even if the child says the dog is hers, and even if you agree that the dog "belongs" to the child, in reality, you are responsible for the care and welfare of the dog. Children will promise anything to get a dog. They'll promise to feed him and brush him and walk him, and they may mean it. In the beginning, they may even do it, but sooner or later, something will come up, and they won't have time or they'll forget. It's up to you to make sure the dog gets his walk or his dinner, no matter where your child is.

A dog is a living entity, not a way to teach your child responsibility. So give your child responsibility, but remember that she is not necessarily going to be able to meet all the dog's needs. Trips to the veterinarian and licensing are two areas beyond the ability of your child. Housetraining may be another area.

The Dachshund makes an ideal apartment dog because of his size and because lots of exercise isn't a requirement.

"Spurlaut" is the high, shrill, distinctive, piercing, and insistent bark of a Dachshund when he spies prey (or something he thinks is prey).

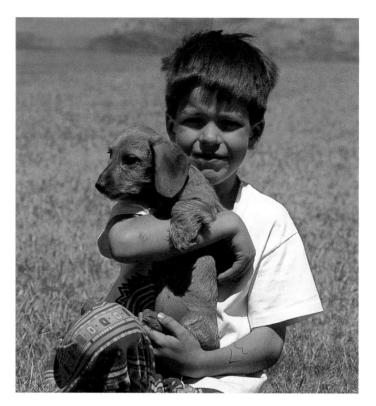

A Dachshund can be an exceptional companion for a child, but remember, responsibility for the dog's daily needs will probably fall to the parents.

Generally speaking, Longhaired Dachshunds are very good with children, Wirehairs are good, and Smooths are fairly good. This is obviously a generalization, but Longhaired Dachshunds tend to be a bit more laid back; the Wires are more playful and ready to go; and the Smooths are a bit more aloof.

A child in school is not going to be able to successfully housetrain a puppy. Housetraining takes patience, persistence, and a parent. Realize that however much the child wants him to be "her" dog, he is also "your" dog. If you are not prepared for that responsibility, you should wait a bit before you add a dog to your home.

Just as some breeders will not sell to anyone with an unfenced yard or a pool, some will not sell to families with small children. Dachshunds can be wonderful with children, but sometimes very small children have a hard time distinguishing between a live puppy and a stuffed toy, and many Dachshunds will take exception to being mauled.

Any Dachshund can be a wonderful dog for a child, but no matter what variety you select there are things to think about: Is your child old enough and mature enough to understand that the puppy you've brought home is a living creature who can be frightened and hurt? Has your child shown that she can be gentle and careful with a puppy? Will there be an adult to supervise interaction between child and dog? Dachshunds are small and can be loving and playful with children, but the general rule is to never, ever leave a

While they will love playing together, puppies—like children— need time to rest.

baby and a dog alone. Babies make sudden movements and high-pitched noises, just like prey. Dogs were, and can still be, predators, especially dogs bred to hunt. Don't *ever* leave a baby and a dog together unattended.

Children have seemingly endless amounts of energy. Puppies may seem very energetic, but they also need their rest. Make sure that your child understands that there is playtime and then there needs to be rest time. Enforce this. Having a crate can make this much simpler. It's easier to pop a tired puppy into a crate and shut the door, letting the child know it's nap time, than to try to convince the child to stop playing with the puppy and let him sleep.

PREPARING
FOR YOUR DACHSHUND

There is no single hard and fast rule for choosing the Dachshund puppy who will be right for you and your family. My best advice is to listen to the breeder or person from whom you are getting your puppy. That person should want the best possible match between puppy and new owner. Just as not every breed is right for every person, not every Dachshund is right for every person. Be honest with your source so that everyone is happy.

WHERE TO FIND YOUR DACHSHUND
Breeders

Because your Dachshund will be a member of the family for 14 to 16 years, take the time to make the right match. Start with finding a breeder you can work with. The Dachshund Club of America has a list of its members online. While there's no guarantee that all the breeders on the list are reputable, the odds are good that they will be. Being a member of the national club means these people have committed a large amount of time and energy to the breed.

Talk to several breeders. A person may be a wonderful breeder, but if you're not comfortable talking with her, find someone else. You want to be able to contact this breeder when you have questions about your Dachshund. The most valuable thing a breeder can give you, besides the puppy, is her phone number—and her time.

Another place to find a breeder is at a dog show. All exhibitors are listed in the back of the catalog, and the list includes their addresses. Talk to the Dachshund people at a show and ask questions about temperament, grooming, exercise. Watch the Dachshunds in the ring. If one catches your eye, maybe you can get a related puppy. Just remember, at a dog show, while you may be able to exchange a word or two ringside before the dog is shown, save the long conversations for after the handler and dog have been in the ring. Before judging, handlers are concentrating on their dog, and may be abrupt if you start asking questions. Talk to them after they've shown and the odds are good they'll be more than happy to help.

Those breeders who breed champions like this dog can tell buyers all about their puppy's ancestry so they know what to expect physically and temperamentally.

Breed Rescue

Rescue organizations are another source to explore. Just because a dog is in rescue doesn't mean there is anything wrong with him. It may be that someone hasn't done the homework necessary for selecting a particular breed of dog. They may have gotten a Dachshund puppy and found he needed more attention than they could give, or the dog needed more exercise than they expected. A divorce may mean the family dog is surrendered to rescue, or someone in the family may be allergic to dogs.

Health Tests for Dachshunds

Hip dysplasia can occur in any breed, and while people tend to think of it as more of a problem in large breeds, it can occur in small breeds as well. Some Dachshund breeders do x-ray their dogs' hips and obtain a rating from the Orthopedic Foundation for Animals (OFA) or from the University of Pennsylvania Hip Improvement Program (PennHip). If this is a concern of yours, choose your puppy from stock that has had its hips tested. Many breeders do thyroid checks on their breeding stock as well. Ask if your puppy's parents have been tested. Did the breeder check the adult Dachshunds' eyes before breeding? With miniature Longhairs, especially, progressive retinal atrophy (PRA) can be a problem. Many breeders of standard Dachshunds will also test for PRA. Some breeders also test for von Willebrands disease, a bleeding disorder.

Questions From a Breeder

Responsible breeders of any breed will ask many questions of prospective buyers, either on the phone, in person, or in writing. Be prepared to honestly answer questions like these:

1. How did you hear about us?
2. How did you become interested in Dachshunds? Do you know someone who owns one?
3. If you own or have owned a Dachshund in the past, please let us know from whom you obtained your dog. If it was some time ago that you had the dog, when was it?
4. Have you read any books about the breed? If so, which ones?
5. What are your expectations for your dog? Pet, show, companion…what words would you use to describe what you would like in a dog?
6. Do you have a preference for a male or a female puppy? Would you take a puppy of the opposite sex should your first choice not be available? If not, what creates the preference?
7. Would you be interested in an older puppy or an adult?
8. Tell us a bit about your household. Do you have a spouse, partner, or roommates? How many children and what are their ages?
9. Do any family members suffer from allergies?
10. Who will be responsible for the care and training of your pet?
11. Would you call your family more the "outdoors-type" or "homebodies"?
12. In what family activities would you include your dog?
13. Have you ever had a dog before? Do you have any pets at this time (other dogs, cats, birds, fish, etc.)? Please tell us a little bit about your previous pet-owning experiences.
14. Do you have a veterinarian your family uses or has used in the past? If yes, please provide the name, address, and telephone number.
15. Do you live in a house, townhouse, condo, or apartment? If so, how large is your yard and what type of fencing do you have?
16. If you rent, are you allowed to have a dog? Please provide the landlord's contact information.
17. Have you thought about how you will handle your dog's exercise needs? Please describe.
18. In what rooms inside your home will your dog be permitted? Do you have any ideas about how you will keep your dog out of certain parts of your home, if necessary?
19. Have you thought about housetraining a puppy and handling an adult dog? Where will your dog go to eliminate? How will you clean up?
20. How many hours each day will your dog be left alone while you're at work? Do you have a secure place to leave your pet while you are away from home? Where will your pet sleep at night?
21. If travel plans took you away from home, what arrangements would you make for your dog? Boarding kennel? Pet sitter? Neighbors or relatives? Take your dog with you?
22. Training and proper socialization are important to a puppy's development into a secure and happy adult companion. Can you devote the time needed during the critical first few months to teach manners and expose your puppy to many new experiences? Do you have any ideas about where you would go for obedience training or socialization?

It's a long list, but you can see that responsible breeders want the best for their puppies, and they want to make sure that you understand exactly what is involved in owning a Dachshund. Answering these questions and reviewing the considerations presented in Chapter 2 will help you to think about your puppy's needs and just how you will meet them. With luck, the puppy you choose will be a loving companion for many years.

As cute as puppies are, there can be advantages to getting an adult, and this is when a rescued dog is especially appropriate. For one thing, an adult will probably, although not always, be housetrained. As adults, they can also wait longer before having to go out. This means you can skip the housetraining stage and may not have to worry as much about accidents in the house. Another advantage to an adult is that he will probably already know some basic commands. He will have outgrown the puppy urge to chew everything in sight. The dog will also be spayed or neutered, as it is very rare for a rescue organization to let any dog go to a new home without this being done.

Conversely, an adult may come with habits or problems that you will have to learn about and deal with. It could be something minor, like having to teach the dog he is no longer allowed on a couch, or it could be something more serious, like a dog who is food aggressive, or is afraid of children. While most rescue organizations have the dogs in foster care to determine just what, if any, problems there might be, animals shelters don't usually have the staff or the time to be able to assess the potential problems. You may trade housetraining time for retraining time.

A rescue organization will ask as many questions as a breeder. They want to find a permanent home for their charges. Don't take offense at these questions. They want the best match possible between dog and family, and they want

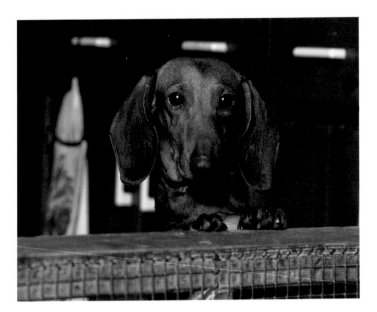

A Dachshund rescue organization may be able to pair you with an older dog who will be just right for you and your family.

the placement to last. A rescue dog may already have been in two or three homes, so the rescuers will be determined to find him a permanent home.

Animal Shelters

Another possible source may be your local animal shelter. Dachshunds are not commonly found in shelters, but it can happen. Many shelters will keep a list of potential adopters, along with their breed preference. If they don't offer such a service, make it a habit to call the shelter once a month or so. You might also want to stop by in person to see the available dogs.

Pet Stores

You may see an adorable Dachshund puppy in the local pet store. Puppies are so hard to resist, but remember, a puppy should not be an impulse purchase. No matter where you get your puppy, there are questions you should ask and papers you should see before you buy a dog who will be a member of your family for many years to come.

For starters, look at the puppies' eyes and noses. Both should be clear, with no discharge. The puppies should be alert and lively. It's all right to feel sorry for the droopy little pup in the corner, but it's probably not the one you should take home. Most breeders give you 48 to 72 hours to have your choice checked by a veterinarian before the sale is final.

You should receive the puppy's pedigree and the registration slip from the seller. If you are buying your puppy from a pet store, ask for these items before you buy the puppy, so that if you have any questions that the store personnel can't answer, you can ask the breeder. Ask about the parents' health clearances as well.

Ask the pet shop to offer that same guarantee. There are lemon laws in many states to assure that you have a healthy dog, but why start out asking for trouble? Take home a healthy pup to begin with. You should also be taking home the health records for that puppy, which should tell you the dates the puppy was wormed and what shots have been given.

Meet one or both of the puppy's parents if possible. It's likely that the puppies will take after them in size and temperament. A shy, fearful mother (dam) or father (sire) is not a good beginning.

How old is the puppy? If he's less than eight weeks, was he taken from his mother too early? If he's older, how much older? A puppy needs socialization, and he may have missed this if he's been in a shop for too long. Ask how he's been socialized and if he's ever been outdoors. If you're getting an older puppy from a breeder, make sure he hasn't spent his life in a kennel but has been around other dogs and people. A Dachshund puppy should love everyone, but he might not if he hasn't had that early socialization.

WAITING FOR THE RIGHT DOG

No matter what source you try, don't expect to get a dog immediately. If you're trying to get a puppy from a breeder, understand that responsible breeders are probably not going to have more than a couple of litters a year. When you call, they may not be planning to have any puppies for six months or more. Also, breeders frequently have waiting lists for their puppies. Even being on a list doesn't guarantee you a puppy. If there are five people waiting and there are only two puppies, three families are going to be disappointed.

Don't be too firm about what you want, either. Don't demand a black female or nothing at all. What if all the girls in the litter are red? What if there are no girls?

There's not much difference between male and female Dachshunds. A male will housetrain as easily as a female but may lift his leg against furniture as a way to mark his territory, especially if exposed to intact females. Neutering at an early age usually (but not always) prevents this. If the dog is a show prospect, you may not neuter while showing, and this means you will have to be ready to deal with this behavior if it starts. With females, unless spayed, you must deal with twice-yearly heat cycles. If you are not planning to

If you're patient and do your homework, when you finally get your Dachshund you'll know you were meant for each other.

show, both sexes should be neutered. This will not affect their personalities and will make them much easier to live with as pets.

Listen to your source and be flexible. I guarantee that dog is going to worm his way into your heart just as quickly whether male or female. Having said that, don't let yourself be talked into a puppy you just don't want. No matter what the outcome of the temperament test or the breeder's assessment of which puppy would be best for your household, if you know you will never be able to deal calmly with a leg-lifting male, hold out for a female. It may mean a longer wait or going to another breeder, but when you choose a puppy, it should be for life.

Pet or Show Quality?

Do you want a pet quality or a show quality puppy? These two terms will likely be in the contract you and the breeder sign. Neither term should have anything to do with health or temperament. Your puppy should be in good health and have the proper Dachshund temperament whether you want a pet or whether you want to show your dog. Calling a dog "show quality" is not a guarantee that the dog will ever become a champion. Show quality means that the dog meets the standard and has no serious faults that

A responsible seller is going to try to make the best match between you and the puppy. It may be that for your lifestyle, the red male is a better match than the black female. A trainer I know once spoke of a particular dog, saying, "Would he be my choice for a family that had never had a dog before? No. Would he be my choice for obedience competition? Absolutely."

Successful show dogs need to look alert and lively in the ring. A dog who hates to show, who lags at the end of the lead, is not going to win, no matter how gorgeous he is physically.

Many people think that if they don't get their puppy as young as possible that the dog won't bond with them. This is not true. Puppies are very adaptable and will quickly adopt and love new humans as quickly as the new humans adopt and love them! As far as that goes, most adult dogs will transfer their love and loyalty to their new family as well, so if you're considering an older rescue dog, don't hesitate because you're afraid you won't bond.

would hinder him from winning. A show-quality Dachshund will have a proper bite, will not be any color that's not allowed, and will otherwise conform to the standard.

A pet-quality Dachshund may have a tail that is set too high. The ears may be set too low or too high. His feet may stick out too far. These things would make it hard, if not impossible, to win in the conformation ring, but none of these would stop the dog from being a loving family companion, or from being able to compete in many of the performance events. A breeder may also call a puppy "pet quality" even if he meets the standard physically if he doesn't have the personality for the conformation ring.

The price for a pet quality puppy is usually less than the price for a show quality puppy. Also, the contract will call for the pet puppy to be spayed or neutered, which helps ensure that a buyer will not breed what a breeder considers a pet quality dog.

No matter what kind of registration the breeder offers, those registration papers should be given to you when you get your puppy. In the United States, the dog will most likely be registered with the AKC, but it might be registered with the United Kennel Club. If your puppy is from Canada, the papers should be from the Canadian Kennel Club. If you're in the UK, the Kennel Club will be the registry. Contact information for these and other registries can be found in the Resources section.

How Old Before He Can Come Home?

The age at which a puppy should go to a new home is a frequently debated question. Many breeders refuse to let a puppy go before eight weeks, and many prefer to keep their puppies until they are twelve weeks old, starting the crate training and housetraining and making sure that the puppies have all necessary vaccinations before they go to their new homes.

READYING YOUR HOME FOR THE NEW ARRIVAL

No matter where you get your Dachshund, make sure you're ready for him before you get him, especially if you're bringing home a puppy. Check electrical cords and tape

No matter what age they are, puppies have no problem bonding with people, so give yours the time he needs with his littermates, and don't rush to bring him home.

them down or tuck them safely away from that inquisitive puppy. Decide what rooms will be off limits. If those rooms don't have doors that you want shut, invest in baby gates for doorways. An adult dog may come with a bed or a crate, but if you're getting a puppy, get a crate before he arrives. Crates are a wonderful way to keep your puppy safe, make housetraining easier, and give your puppy his own little den.

Beds

There are so many wonderful types of dog beds on the market that you'll be tempted to buy several. Until your Dachshund is an adult, however, you might want to stick with old towels or flannel sheets. These can make a perfectly wonderful, cozy, warm bed. They are also inexpensive, so if your Dachshund decides to chew them, you won't be out a lot of money—and you won't be angry at your puppy; after all, he's just being a dog. Towels and flannel sheets are easy to wash, and puppies are likely to have accidents. Many beds are washable, but drying a foam bed can take hours. Even with a dryer, many won't dry completely and need to be air-dried for two or three days. Crates can make great beds that double as a den, too. They'll be discussed in greater detail later in the chapter.

Regardless of the type of bed you choose for your Dachshund, it's a good idea to put them in places where it'll be convenient and practical for your friend to use them.

Make your dog's sleeping areas practical and comfortable so you don't risk something fancy getting soiled or chewed.

That means putting beds in places you frequent with your family—the kitchen, the den, and of course, your bedroom. Unless you are vehemently opposed to your Dachshund sleeping in the same room with you, you will all be happier with him there. With his own comfy spot, he won't be tempted to join you in your bed.

Collars and Leashes

These are absolute necessities, and before you buy something purely because it looks nice, remember that these items must be functional as well as attractive. Collars that are too heavy or bulky may even harm your puppy or dog. Leashes that slip out of your hand, are too thin or too thick or too fancy will soon have you frustrated when you need to simply control your dog on a walk.

Remember, too, that your puppy will grow. You may want to outfit him in a cheaper nylon collar until he's reached his adult size and you can invest in a leather collar that may last the rest of his life. Many puppy collars today are made so that the buckle tongue can be pushed through the fabric at any point, making it easy to expand the collar as the puppy grows.

Measure your puppy's neck before you buy a collar, or, better yet, bring him along to the pet supply store so you can select one that meets all your criteria right away. The same goes for a leash. Look at the different sizes and styles and "test drive" the ones you like. A basic 6-foot leash made of cotton, nylon, or leather is a safe selection.

Keep your dog's bedding clean. Wash it separately as often as you wash your own linens to keep them clean. Your dog may not care, but you'll notice a difference.

Identification Tags and Licenses

Most places don't require your dog to have a license until he's six months old, but you'll want to put an identification tag on the collar immediately. The tag should list your dog's name and your phone number. Select a material that won't wear down too easily and a design that will properly secure to the collar. Eventually your dog will have his ID tag, license, and rabies tag together on the collar. You can buy tag silencer pouches now that keep the jingle of multiple tags to a minimum.

As important as a clear ID tag is, any or all tags could come off or be removed from a dog's collar. A permanent way to identify your dog is by having him tattooed and/or microchipped. Dogs can be tattooed with a special number that's put on the inside of their thigh or ear. They can also get a microchip implanted in the muscle between their shoulder blades. The microchip is about the size of a grain of rice and contains a special number that belongs to your dog. A special scanner can read the number and then a veterinarian or shelter worker can check with the microchip registry and locate you. Do use some form of identification. If your Dachshund should get lost, that identification chip may mean the difference between that loss being permanent or getting your dog back.

Food and Water Bowls

Invest in a good set of dishes—ones that are easy to clean, won't slip when you put them on the floor, and aren't made of potentially harmful materials. Stainless steel is relatively inexpensive and can be thoroughly cleaned. The stainless steel food and water bowls are typically lined with rubber on the bottom to prevent skidding. There are lots of adorable ceramic bowls out there, too, but just be sure that the paint or glaze is not lead based. Hard plastic is not a great choice because it may be chewed on and possibly swallowed. In addition to being destroyed, it may also harbor germs, and the material itself can become toxic over time.

Your dog will need one bowl for food and a separate bowl for water. The bowls should be cleaned before and after use, just as yours are. Cool, clean water should be offered at all times, and the water should be changed several times a day.

Toys and Chews

Because puppies love to play and chew, you should get toys that are appropriate for the size of the puppy. A toy that's too small can get stuck in a dog's throat. A toy that's too big may not be easily enjoyed. My dogs have always loved stuffed toys with squeakers, but they also love ripping the toy open to get at the squeaker. I have to supervise play so that when the toy is torn open, I'm there to remove all the stuffing. I don't want the dogs swallowing mouthfuls of that synthetic fiber. So, I pull it all out and the dogs get the "shell" of the toy, the outer fabric cover. Some dogs never destroy a stuffed toy and will carry it around for years. Just keep an eye on your dog until you know which kind he is.

Dachshunds are notorious chewers, and their desire to chew needs to be satisfied. If you don't choose something appropriate, your dog will choose something inappropriate. Hard nylon and rubber chews can often keep a Dachshund occupied for hours at a time. Nylabones are recommended by breeders and veterinarians for active chewers. There are even toys you

Puppies enjoy chewing on rope toys and other appropriate chews.

can stuff with goodies that make them even more appealing. Rotate your Dachshund's toys and chews, too, so he doesn't get bored.

Just remember to supervise play and make sure toys don't have any sharp parts. If it's a stuffed toy, check any added parts, like floppy ears or bows. Keep playtime safe and happy.

REGISTERING YOUR DOG

A purebred dog is eligible for American Kennel Club registration if his litter has been registered. When you purchase a dog said to be AKC-registrable, you should get an individual registration application from the seller. Once the application has been completed, you should submit it to the AKC with the proper fee. You will receive your dog's AKC registration certificate in about one week. This must be filled out jointly by the litter owner and the new owner of the dog. The application is color-coded for the convenience of both parties. The litter owner must fill out most of the application, including the sex of the dog; color and markings; type of registration (either full or limited); date of transfer; the name and address of the new owner or owners and any co-owners; and the litter owner or owners must sign the form.

As the new owner of the dog, you must supply the name of the dog, sign the form, note method of payment, and check any options you may want, such as your dog's official

AKC pedigree or any videos. When the application has been received and processed by the AKC, the registration certificate will be mailed to you. Examine it carefully and report any errors to the AKC.

Each person or firm who owns, breeds, or sells dogs who are AKC-registrable must keep accurate, up-to-date records of all transactions involving the dogs. There must be no doubt as to the identity of any individual dog or as to the parentage of a particular dog or litter.

Dogs from other countries may be registered with the AKC, provided the dog is registered with another recognized kennel club. For instance, a Canadian dog must have an unrestricted registration with the Canadian Kennel Club. A transfer of ownership on the AKC's records will only be affected after it is documented that the same change has been made by the registry organization in the owner's country of residence. Application for a foreign-bred dog must be accompanied by an official three-generation pedigree.

The Benefits of Registration

Of course, your Dachshund will still be your loyal pal whether you manage to register him or not, but if you are planning to compete in any AKC events, he'll need to be registered. It's easier and cheaper to register your Dachshund when you first get him. Then, if you do decide to compete or do more with your Dachshund than just have him as a companion, you'll be ready.

Registering in the UK

The registration process with the Kennel Club is similar to that of the AKC. If a breeder has a litter to register, he contacts the Kennel Club or downloads the necessary form

What's an ILP?

If you have a Dachshund but don't have any papers because you got the dog at a shelter or through a rescue group, but you still want to compete in AKC performance events, you may apply for an ILP number. ILP stands for Indefinite Listing Privilege. You won't be able to enter conformation shows, but with an ILP number you can compete in any other AKC event. You'll need to take pictures of your Dachshund to send in along with the application form and fee so that the AKC representatives are assured that your dog is, in fact, a Dachshund.

from the Kennel Club website. After completing the form and sending it with the proper fee to the Kennel Club, the breeder will receive a litter registration certificate and one registration certificate for each puppy in the litter. When the breeder sells a puppy, she signs and dates the Breeder Registration Certificate and gives it to the new owner with other documentation. The breeder should encourage the new owner to complete the Change of Ownership and return it to the Kennel Club. After the new owner has sent in the paperwork, The Kennel Club sends back a registration certificate and a booklet, *Giving Dogs a Good Home*, which provides general information on the Kennel Club and the world of dogs.

TRAVELING WITH YOUR DACHSHUND

Whether it's a trip to the store or a trip across the country, traveling with your Dachshund should be enjoyable for everyone. Most enjoy a ride in the car, although some may get a bit carsick as puppies. Carry a roll of paper towels with you and you can easily clean up after the little one.

To ensure that your pet will always be a willing traveler, start when he's a puppy to get him used to the car. Take him for short rides that don't always end at the veterinarian's office. How eager would you be to get in the car if you always ended up at the doctor's office? Take the puppy with you when you drop off the kids at school as well. Not only will this be a happy car ride, it's a good way to socialize the puppy at the same time. Any time you can take the dog with you, do it. Reward him with treats when he jumps in the car. Soon you'll have a dog who begs to go with you every time you pick up your car keys.

Putting your Dachshund in a crate for car rides will help keep him safe, but there are other ways to restrain your dog in the car, including special harnesses that attach to the seat belt. What you use is your choice, but use something. Dogs riding loose in the car can distract the driver, and Dachshunds are small enough to get between the driver's feet and the pedals. In an accident, a Dachshund can be seriously injured, and if not injured in the actual crash, he may escape from the car into traffic. Even if there's not an accident, Dachshunds are quick. Open the door for just a minute to run into the store, and your Dachshund may be

Beware a Hot Car

When the sun is shining, the interior of a closed car can reach dangerously high temperatures very quickly. Never take your dog with you if he's going to have to stay in a closed car for very long. Even in the fall and spring, when the outdoor temperature may seem pleasant, if the sun is shining, the inside of the car can reach lethal temperatures. Parking in the shade may not help because as the sun moves, your car may no longer be in the shade. Windows can't safely be left open very far if your dog is loose in the car; Dachshunds can get through surprisingly small openings, and they will. Even if your dog is crated, you might not want your windows all the way down. So, think ahead. If there's even a chance that the dog will be left in a hot car, leave him at home.

right beside you or out in the middle of the road. Restrain your Dachshund for safety.

Vacation Considerations

When vacation time rolls around, it will be time to decide if you want to take your Dachshund along, board him, or use a pet sitter. If you're driving and you want to have your dog with you, plan ahead. Will the dog be allowed at your destination? Will the dog be allowed at any of the places you may be stopping along the way? If there will be overnight stays at motels, call ahead and make sure your pet will be welcome. Some motels will charge an extra fee for a pet. The fee may or may not be refundable. Some motels will agree to a dog if the dog will be crated and if he is never left in the room unattended. Find out what the rules are before you arrive at the motel. The advent of the Internet has made checking out various motels much easier, faster, and cheaper.

If you're planning on stopping at attractions during the trip, call ahead on those, too. Many large parks have kennel facilities. Otherwise, think about where your dog will be while you're enjoying the water slide. Remember, leaving the dog locked in a hot car is *not* an option. If your entire vacation is going to be visits to parks and museums, a boarding kennel or pet sitter may be a better idea for your Dachshund.

If your travel plans include camping, make sure your campground accepts dogs. Find out the rules *before* you go.

Packing for Your Dog

If your dog will be traveling with you, you'll need to pack for him as well as for the family. Take a small first-aid kit, as well as some water for your dog. If you'll be on the road longer than a few days, mix local water with your dog's water so he gets used to the change gradually. Carry dog food. Unless you're absolutely sure it is a kind you can get at your destination, make sure you carry enough for the entire trip. Suddenly changing foods on top of the stress of traveling can lead to digestive upsets.

Make sure your dog is wearing a collar and tags. If you're going to be at your destination for a week or more, you might want to have a tag made with the local phone number on it, or the number of someone who will know how to reach you no matter where you are in your travels. Carry your dog's rabies certificate and proof of vaccinations. If your dog is on any medication at all, take enough to last for the length of the trip. If you give heartworm medicine each month, carry it with you. Do you use a monthly flea preventative? Add that to your bag.

I always carry extra towels. Dachshunds love splashing through puddles, and because they're short, this means that their undersides get as dirty as their paws. A few extra towels can protect your car and your clothes. Towels make good beds, too. If you don't want to carry food bowls, a paper plate works just fine and can be thrown away instead of being washed.

Carry cleanup materials with you at all times and *pick up after your dog.* No one, not even another dog lover, wants to step in a mess left by your dog. Pick it up. There are all kinds of products on the market that make this easy. There's even one that fastens onto your dog's lead. With Dachshunds, a small plastic sandwich bag works just fine. Turn it inside out over your hand, pick up the waste, pull the bag forward over

Your Dog's Travel Kit

My dogs' travel bag contains a couple of inexpensive dog bowls, a couple of toys, dog treats, a long lead for exercise if there's a large open space, and two old sheets for covering the beds in motel rooms. When we're at home, the dogs don't sleep on the beds, but when we travel, they love to jump up and be with us while we're reading or watching television. Rugs can be vacuumed, but bedspreads are not washed after every guest, and dog hairs have a way of working into the threads of a bedspread. Be considerate and spread out a towel or sheet. This also prevents mud and water from being transferred from your Dachshund to the bedspread. If you don't want to carry your own, ask the housekeeping staff for a sheet. They'd rather launder an extra sheet or two than have to deal with a hairy bedspread.

Your dog's crate and collar with identification tags are some of the staples you'll need before setting off on a trip together.

it, twist shut, and deposit in the nearest trash receptacle. There are even some biodegradable bags on the market that may be safely flushed.

I also travel with a lightweight folding crate for each dog. The hard-sided crates stay in the car for travel, and the mesh crates go into the motel room. They're much lighter and easier to carry, especially if you're on the second floor and there's no elevator. A few towels on the floor of the crate make it cozy, and your dog has a safe spot when you're not in the room. Crating your dog in a motel room is a good way to prevent any damage to the room. A piece of plastic under the crate, or at least under the food and water dishes, will cut down on stains from any accidental spills.

I can't stress enough the need to leave your dog crated in a motel room, but I also know that on rare occasions, there will be a dog who just can't tolerate a crate. If that's the case, put out the "do not disturb" sign. You don't want someone coming to clean your room and letting your dog escape. You also don't want your dog barking or growling at whoever opens the door.

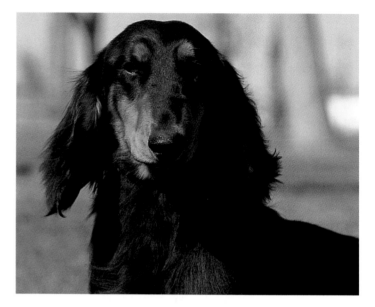

To keep your Dachshund looking and smelling his best during your travels, be sure to pack towels and other clean-up items.

Flying With Your Dog

You may, of course, be flying to your vacation destination, and that requires different thought. Every airline is different, and the rules change frequently, so check with your specific carrier, so there'll be no surprises. All airlines have limits on when they will fly dogs as cargo and some may have a limit as to how many they will accept on any given flight.

If your dog will be flying as baggage, you will need an airline-approved crate. Plastic may be a better bet than metal because metal tends to absorb more heat. Tape a label on the crate that lists destination, your name, address and telephone number, and the dog's name. You might also want to include your veterinarian's phone number. Make sure there is absorbent bedding in the crate. Shredded paper is a good choice. Freeze water in the water dish so that your dog can either lick the ice, or drink the water as the ice melts.

Making a Home Away From Home

If you must leave the dog in the room alone, turn on a radio or television. This will mask noises that might otherwise cause your dog to bark. No one wants to listen to your dog bark while you're out enjoying yourself. My dogs are very good about being left alone, but I did have one once who was not so good. She frequently barked when left alone. Our solution was to take her with us when we went out to dinner. Of course, if you have a barker and the weather is hot, dinner will have to be the drive-thru window of a fast food restaurant.

This prevents the water supply from spilling all at once. You may also want to run a bungee cord over the door to prevent it from opening if the crate is dropped.

Check with airline personnel about how and when your dog will be loaded and where and when you can pick him up when the flight lands. Plan your route carefully. Plane transfers will be harder on your dog, especially if the plane heats up or the crate is left on the blacktop in the sun. There is also more of a chance that he can get lost en route. If you are traveling in very hot weather, the airline may refuse to fly your dog at all. The optimal temperature range, and frequently the range the airlines use, is 45°F to 85°F. If it will be colder than 45°F or warmer than 85°F at either the originating airport or your destination, or anyplace in between that the plane may land, most airlines will refuse to ship your dog.

If you don't actually see your dog being boarded, ask the gate counter agent to call the ramp to make sure your dog is on board. Pick up the dog promptly at your destination. If you don't get your dog in a reasonable amount of time, ask about him. Ask before your plane has taken off again.

If you're staying more than a night or two in a hotel, you should consider tipping the housekeeper at the beginning of your stay rather than at the end. This can make whoever cleans your room a bit happier, or at least a bit more willing to vacuum up those Dachshund hairs—and let's face it, there will be Dachshund hairs.

Bringing Minis On Board

Most miniature Dachshunds are small enough for soft carriers that will fit under the seat in the cabin. Airlines generally limit the number of live animals they will allow in the passenger section, and they charge for this service, so make your arrangements ahead of time. Don't just arrive at the airport with your dog in his carrier.

If you've decided that you do want to try to take your dog on the plane with you, make sure he's used to the carrier before the trip. Feed him in the carrier and take him on short car rides while he's in it. If he's crate trained, you shouldn't have too much trouble, but the soft dog carriers are smaller than crates, so there will be a bit of adjustment necessary.

Choosing and Using a Boarding Kennel

I love having my dogs with me, but sometimes I want the freedom to sightsee without having to get back to feed or exercise them. I want to stay up late and not have to get out of bed at 6 a.m. to walk the dogs. That's when I make arrangements for my dogs to stay at a boarding kennel. If you do your homework, you should have no qualms about leaving your dog behind at a kennel. Sure, they'd rather be with you, but they'll be safe and well cared for in a kennel.

This does not mean that you don't still have some work to do before you leave your dog. Visit the kennel ahead of time. Take note of the fencing and the runs. The fencing should be in good repair, with no bent pieces of wire that could injure a Dachshund. The runs should be clean. There may be a doggy odor or the odor of a cleaning product, but it shouldn't smell of urine or feces. There should be water in the runs. If there are dishes in the runs, what do they look like? Are they clean?

I prefer a kennel where the walls separating the runs are solid on the bottom to prevent contact between the dogs, but I would not reject a kennel where the runs were separated only by chain-link fencing, if everything else met with my approval. Ask about drop-off and pick-up times. For an extra fee, some kennels offer a pickup and delivery service. Do they give baths? Dogs pick up a definite kennel odor with an extended stay at a kennel. I like mine to get a bath and have their nails trimmed before they come home.

Many kennels have an exercise yard where dogs have more room than in their run. If you have more than one dog, this gives them a chance to play together. Ask about the kennel's policy regarding putting strange dogs together. Many dogs get along quite well, but if you don't want your dog socializing with others, or you know your dog doesn't get along with other dogs, tell the operator. It's always better to supply too much information, rather than too little.

Specific Concerns

Some kennels will also offer extras in the way of individual walks on lead and possibly basic training. If you have a very active Dachshund, a daily walk might be a good idea.

Will the staff give your dog any necessary medications? There may be an extra charge for this. What do they do in an emergency? Most kennels will ask for your veterinarian's name, but in an emergency, they may use one they know or someone closer to the kennel. Tell them your preference. When I board our dogs I always request that any problem be

Your dog may look pathetic when you leave him at the kennel, but harden your heart and walk away. The odds are good that he'll quickly adjust, and if the kennel operator offers a dog biscuit or two, your Dachshund will make a new friend in record time.

treated aggressively. I would rather pay a veterinary bill for a false alarm than have something serious overlooked.

Once you've chosen a kennel, it might be a good idea to plan a short practice visit for your dog. Board your dog for a couple of nights. This will give your dog a chance to get to know the kennel and the kennel operator, and your dog will also learn that you will return. Also, the younger your dog is, the more easily he will adapt to a kennel. A dog who is 10 or 12 years old the first time he is boarded is not going to adjust as quickly as a young dog.

If you have more than one dog, many kennels will let your dogs share a run, often at a reduced price. If you decide on this option, make sure your dogs will get along together if they are fed in the confined area of a run. Possibly the kennel operator will agree to feeding them separately. Again, find out ahead of time.

To Bring or Not to Bring

You may want to take your dog's crate to put into the run, especially if the runs do not have a solid barrier between them. That way your dog can have a private space, which may help until he adjusts to the kennel. Many people like to take their dog's bed to a kennel, and it's a nice thought. My recommendation is an old blanket or rug you don't care about, or several old bath towels. These items can be easily washed, and if the dog destroys them, it's no great loss. I've seen lovely, expensive wicker baskets, as well as bean bag

Most kennels allow pairs of dogs to share a run and spend their time together.

beds and beds stuffed with foam, be totally destroyed. An anxious dog may be a destructive dog.

The kennel will supply the dishes and water pails, so leave yours at home. The kennel owner has probably already chosen a dry food that seems to agree with most dogs. If your dog is on a special diet, or you don't want him to change foods while being boarded, most operators will allow you to supply your own food. Do not expect a discount for this. Food is a very minor part of what you're paying for, and as a former kennel owner, I know that it is much easier to feed everyone the same food, rather than fixing several dogs special meals, especially if that special meal includes dry and canned food, supplements, hard boiled eggs, and other items. I was always willing to do whatever the owner wanted to keep the dog happy and healthy, and most kennel operators feel the same, but to suggest they take less money for more work is not appropriate.

Pet Sitters

Another option is to hire a pet sitter. With a pet sitter, your dog remains in your home. He is familiar with the house and yard, and especially for an older dog, there will be less stress. Pet sitters will come in from two to five times a day for varying lengths of time. They will walk your dog at your request or play with the dog for a few minutes. Pet sitters are more expensive than a boarding kennel, but there is the advantage that someone is in and out of your home, possibly even watering your plants and bringing in your mail. Most importantly, your dog will be in familiar surroundings. If you have an old dog or a dog with any medical problems, using a pet sitter might be a better choice than a boarding kennel.

As with a boarding kennel, if you want to use a pet sitter, make arrangements before you need them. Talk to sitters about the times you would expect them to visit. Find out how they handle emergencies. Are they willing to give medications? What experience have they had, and with what kinds of dogs? Check references. Once you have settled on a sitter, have her visit your home to meet your dog *before* you go away. Two or three meetings are even better. You want both your dog and the sitter to be comfortable with each other.

No matter what option you choose, keep your dog's health and safety in mind when you're planning your vacation.

While the idea of your dog having his favorite toy with him is a comforting thought, for the most part, dogs in kennels don't play with their toys much. Also, a toy or bone that is fine at home where you are supervising your dog may not be a good idea in a kennel run. Most people who run kennels will remove anything they consider unsafe, but it's your decision. If the toy or bone is questionable, leave it at home.

FEEDING
YOUR DACHSHUND

Food is a very important part of your Dachshund's life, as he'll be sure to let you know! But no dog can choose his own diet, and it's up to you to make sure you feed your Dachshund the very best in nutrition, keeping him healthy and helping him reach his optimum age.

There was a time when no commercial dog foods were available. Dogs lived on what their people lived on. They ate table scraps and the occasional bone from the butcher. There was no specific balanced diet for dogs. Now, the grocery aisles are lined with all kinds of dog foods and treats. Our dogs eat balanced meals every day, and the diet is consistent. Interestingly, some people now advocate the earlier type of diet, with daily variety, raw bones, and even more "people" food.

With all the choices today, what is the best food? The grocery store shelves are full of all kinds of dog foods in all different forms. There are big bags of dry food, packets of semi-moist foods, and rows and rows of canned food. Beyond that, many dog owners prefer cooking for their dogs, and many more have chosen to follow the BARF diet, which stands for Bones And Raw Food, or Biologically Appropriate Raw Food.

Your puppy's breeder probably gave you information about your puppy's diet and, at first, you should follow those guidelines. If your breeder is feeding a premium dry dog food, you will, too. If she prefers canned, or raw, or home-cooked food, she's probably given you information to help you do the same. As your dog grows, you may find you want to try something else.

Whatever you feed, make sure you understand what your dog needs to stay healthy, and what specific diets require. Also, when changing foods, do it gradually, over a period of about a week, to prevent stomach upsets or diarrhea. (The exception to this may be if you are switching from commercial to a BARF diet, when a clean break may be preferred.)

MEETING DOG FOOD STANDARDS

All commercial food, whether dry, canned, or semi-moist, must meet AAFCO standards. AAFCO stands for the American Association of Feed Control Officials, and it is

Your Dachshund will look forward to his meals, and with all the kinds of foods available today, it's important that you choose what's best for your dog.

the governing body for all animal feed products and sets strict guidelines and procedures.

AAFCO provides a system for developing and implementing uniform and equitable laws, regulations, standards, and enforcement policies for the manufacture, labeling, distribution, and sale of animal feeds. The Agriculture Department of all 50 states of the United States requires AAFCO compliance with regard to manufacturing and labeling. This prevents false claims or statements and prevents the distribution of "noncompliant" feeds.

Just because a food meets AAFCO standards doesn't mean there isn't some comparison-shopping to be done. Read the label and check the list of ingredients. Two of the first five ingredients should be an animal-based protein and, ideally, one of those should be in the first position. Chicken, beef, and lamb are the usual kinds of meat you'll find listed. Next, how much filler is there? Corn is cheap, but many dogs are allergic to corn. One breeder I know stays away from any

Your Dog's Response to Food

Observe your dog and see how he responds to his food. Does he eat it quickly and seem to enjoy it? Check his stools: Are they firm? Is his coat in good condition, or is it dull or brittle? No matter Ahat type of coat your dog has—Long, Smooth, or Wire—your Dachshund's coat should have the luster of good health.

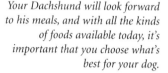

product with wheat in it, but I look for wheat, rather than corn. Some dogs react to soy. This will be trial and error, but it is something to be alert to.

Another thing to pay attention to when selecting a food is the type of preservative used. Many people look for a food preserved with vitamin E (listed as tocopherol). What you need to remember about "natural" preservatives is that they will not preserve the food as long as some other preservatives, so you will want to buy smaller quantities of the food.

Look to see if the dog food you're choosing contains "meat by-products." This may sound unappealing, but, in fact, may be very good for dogs. Meat by-products are the lungs, liver, kidneys, spleen, heart, brains, intestines, stomach, etc.—the organs that are always the first to be eaten by wild dogs and cats. Chicken by-products also include the head and feet of the bird. Organ meats are extremely high in natural vitamins and minerals. By law, meat by-products in dog food do not include hair, horn, teeth or hooves, feathers or manure. Many people prefer to feed only real meat to their dogs, but by-products don't necessarily indicate poor ingredients.

If your dog is scratching, if his skin seems dry and flaky, or if he is chewing at his paws, he may be allergic to something in his food. A trip to the veterinarian will rule out other causes, and if it appears that a food allergy is the problem, your veterinarian will help you determine what the source is.

COMMERCIAL DOG FOOD OPTIONS

Commercial food offers several options to the dog owner. Dry food is the most convenient, economical, and sound choice and should be the base of your Dachshund's diet. Dry food (kibble) gives dogs something hard to chew, which helps keep the dog's teeth clean, though most dogs tend to gulp their food rather than do any sustained chewing. The advantage to dry food is that it will not stick to the teeth as easily as semi-moist or canned, thus keeping the dog's mouth a bit cleaner.

Semi-moist food is more expensive than dry. It is soft and frequently molded into shapes designed to please people. Some of it may look like ground meat because of added dyes. Read the label. It may meet AAFCO nutritional standards, but it may also contain more of the things you may want to avoid, like preservatives and sugars and starches, which are added for texture, flavor, and aroma.

Canned food is the most expensive choice, but it contains more meat, and most dogs find the smell, texture, and taste

Puppies weaned on softened kibble have no problem adjusting to regular kibble, which makes for a nutritionally sound food base.

irresistible. But again, read the label. How much of what is in the can is just filler? Many owners mix a small amount of canned food with a base of kibble so their dogs are getting a nutritionally sound meal with the added bonus of tasty canned food.

Premium dog foods offer a balanced diet for your dog, with necessary vitamins and minerals. If you feed a balanced food, you shouldn't need supplements. Commercially prepared foods are the easiest, cheapest way to feed your Dachshund.

Assessing Brands

There are dozens of brands of dog food on the market, and while many are high quality, not all are right for every dog. Even within a breed, one brand may be too rich for an individual dog, or not be well tolerated by a dog. If you plan to feed a commercial diet, study the labels, ask your breeder, ask friends, and observe your dog. If he is not itching or chewing on himself, if his coat is glossy and healthy-looking, if he is growing well and is not too fat or too thin, and if his stools are small and firm, chances are you're feeding him an appropriate food.

NON-COMMERCIAL DIET OPTIONS

All-natural diets are gaining in popularity, as are home-cooked meals. If you decide to prepare your Dachshund's food yourself, be aware that he still needs a balanced diet. Cooking up some ground meat or chicken and adding some boiled rice may be fine to help correct the occasional upset stomach, but it is not a balanced diet. Bones with the meat attached are not balanced. And, there is a concern about bacteria in raw meat and eggs, and about splintering and other effects from bones. Some veterinarians are totally against feeding raw meat because of the health threat of salmonella and *E. coli*; others say that the benefits outweigh the possible danger. People who feed raw claim their dogs have shinier coats, cleaner teeth, and fewer health problems.

Very few dogs have problems with fresh bones, but some do, and pounding or grinding the bones can help prevent problems.

Cooking for Your Dog

Cooking for your dog and meeting nutritional standards means adding vegetables as well as vitamins and minerals. There are some excellent books on the subject of natural feeding versus commercial foods. If this is what you prefer, research the subject thoroughly. Two books that will help are *Give Your Dog a Bone,* by Dr. Ian Billinghurst, and *Raw Dog Food*, by Carina Beth MacDonald.

Your veterinarian may not approve of a raw diet, but see if he or she will work with you anyway. Suggest a blood scan before you switch your dog to raw, and then test every six months or so to determine that balances are correct. You don't want to lose a good veterinarian over this issue, and requesting the blood tests may help to keep your veterinarian in your corner.

Talk to an animal nutritionist if you are serious about cooking for your dog. Make sure you have the freezer and refrigerator room, too. If you only have one or two Dachshunds, either standard or miniature, just the freezer that is part of your refrigerator ought to be fine, but many people who feed raw like the convenience of a larger freezer because it enables them to take advantage of sales on bones and raw foods. One veterinarian who feeds and recommends raw, though, also recommends pounding or grinding all bones.

Keep in mind that the key to feeding bones is that they are raw and fresh! Cooked bones are bad for dogs. They are hard and brittle, and poultry bones, especially, can splinter and pierce a dog's stomach or intestines. Many raw food diets suggest recreational bones for your dog to gnaw on,

Taking a Special Diet on the Road

If you're traveling with your dog, carry a cooler, or plan to buy fresh meat as you travel. It takes a bit more effort than a commercial food, but it can be done. If you supply daily packets of your dog's food, most boarding kennels should be willing to continue your dog's raw diet. This is something to find out about ahead of time. Nobody likes surprises, so don't just show up at your boarding kennel with your raw food, and don't be disappointed if the kennel operator refuses to feed the bones. Settle everything ahead of time.

but it's important not to let these bones just lay around the yard for days at a time. After a day or two, these bones will dry out and become as much of a problem as cooked bones. The meat and bones you feed your Dachshund should also be organic, especially with a raw diet.

While commercial foods are certainly fast and easy, feeding raw doesn't have to take up inordinate amounts of time. For instance, you can make up enough of your vegetable mixture to last a week or two, and then freeze it in daily amounts in small containers. If your dog eats three chicken necks a day, buy enough for a week or two, make up packets for each day, and take them out of the freezer as needed.

VARYING YOUR DOG'S DIET

There's another school of thought that says that no matter what you feed your dog, there should be variety. Our dogs shouldn't eat the same food day in and day out. One of the reasons that a food change should be done gradually, over a week or so, is because of the habit of feeding one food constantly. If you know any vegetarians, you'll know that they get physically ill if they eat meat. That's because their system hasn't experienced meat in so long that it doesn't know how to deal with it. I've read that deer herds can starve to death in a bad winter even if food is provided, because it is not food they are used to.

Veterinarian Wendy Blount notes that, "we know that digestive enzymes are induced by foods found in the digestive tract. It's quite possible that dogs get diarrhea when we change their diet just because we ruin their ability to digest a variety of foods by feeding only a single type food. If you ate only biscuits and chicken every day for three years, you'd probably be doubled over in pain if you ate an orange, which is full of wonderful nutrients. Oranges causing pain doesn't mean that oranges are bad for you—just the opposite, you should eat them more often. I have German Shepherds, a breed notorious for their sensitive GI tracts. Every time I open a new bag of dog food, it's a different brand and flavor than the last. And every night I open a can of food that is different than the night before. They get a variety of fresh foods as a "top dressing." I have a list of several dozen varieties of kibble and canned foods I rotate through—all whole foods with no chemical preservatives."

I can't tell you what is right or wrong for your dog. That's going to depend on your lifestyle and on what you learn from your breeder, your veterinarian and other Dachshund owners.

YOUR DOG'S DISHES

Whatever food you choose, feed your dog from a clean dish and make sure he always has access to fresh, clean water. The kind of dish is important. You want to choose something that is durable, easy to clean, and doesn't slip. Stainless steel and heavy ceramic are the best choices. However, if you decide on that adorable ceramic bowl decorated with bones, make sure the paint and glaze are lead-free.

I like a dish that is lighter weight and non-breakable, but that's just a personal preference. No matter what kind of

Your Dachshund will need to have a ready supply of cool, fresh water in an easy-to-clean, durable bowl.

dish you use, make sure you wash it after every meal. Just because your dog has licked the bowl clean doesn't mean it is clean. You wouldn't use your dinner dishes over and over without washing them.

If you have more than one dog, you will need to monitor them at meal times so that there's no argument over the food. Don't put the bowls down side by side, but a few feet in between should be acceptable for all. You don't want the dominant dog to get all the food, and you certainly don't want a dogfight. If eating together doesn't work with your dogs, you'll need to separate them. Feeding in separate areas, or in crates, also ensures that each dog gets whatever may be added to his food, like a supplement or a medicine. When dogs are fed separately, you can tell if one is off his food, or hasn't eaten his heartworm pill. If you're feeding raw, this also gives each dog a chance to really chew the bones, instead of gulping everything.

Dachshunds are always willing to eat, so if you asked him how often he wanted to eat, your Dachsie would probably say hourly. Good thing you're in charge of feeding him! Adult dogs should be fed either once or twice a day, though most people find twice a day preferable. Puppies, of course, get four meals a day when they're first weaned off their mother's milk, then three, and, by about the age of six months, twice a day.

Another option is to free-feed your dog, which means that you put down the daily food and it's there all day, whenever your dog wants to eat it. In a multiple-dog household, this simply won't work, because one of the dogs will eat more than his share. If you only have one dog, you can try this, but with a Dachshund, chances are all the food will be gone in the first few minutes.

Other problems with free feeding are that if you are trying to give any kind of medication with the food, you'll want that medication given at specific times; also, you won't be as aware of your dog's appetite, which is one of the first indicators that your dog is not feeling well.

HOW MUCH TO FEED

How much you feed your dog will depend on his activity level and age. Puppies will eat more than your average adult, and an active adult will eat more than the older couch potato.

Most dog foods have a recommended amount for feeding, but you'll want to talk to other Dachshund owners and adjust that amount for your Dachshund. The amount you feed will also depend on whether you have a standard or a miniature Dachshund.

Typically, standard puppies should be fed about $1/2$ cup of kibble with a teaspoon of canned food four times a day. Reduce that to three feedings a day at about 16 weeks of age, then cut back to two feedings a day by four months. Miniature Dachshunds will need about half that amount.

If you feed raw, the recommended amount of raw meaty bones is two to three per cent of your dog's body weight. Dogs on the BARF diet are fed twice daily because the morning meal is always the raw, meaty bones, and the evening meal is a vegetable mix, with muscle meat or organ meat.

Every Dachshund is different, and it's up to you to feed your dog what he needs—neither too little nor too much.

AGE-APPROPRIATE FEEDING

You'll want to feed your puppy a premium puppy food for his first few months, switching to an adult food when he is about six months old. If you plan to feed raw, you might want to pound or grind the bones until your Dachshund is an adult.

Adult dog foods come with varying levels of protein and fat, but all are geared for an active, healthy adult. If you're doing a lot of activities with your dog, you may want a food with a higher level of protein. Talk to your breeder about this, as well as your veterinarian.

Senior dogs (those seven to eight years old or older) start to slow down, just like people. They may not want to walk as far, and they tend to take more naps. It may be that the food that has kept your Dachshund healthy all these years is now too rich, or isn't being digested as well. You should consider feeding a senior formula, which has a lower level of protein and may contain beneficial supplements like glucosamine and chondroitin for stiffening joints, or other vitamins/minerals, foods, or herbs.

DON'T LET YOUR DACHSHUND GET FAT

No matter what kind of food you give your Dachshund, obesity can be a problem. Dachshunds love to eat, and they are very good at persuading you that they are starving. It's so hard to resist those big brown eyes and that cute face. For

A Sample Raw Diet

To get a sense of what goes into feeding a raw diet, here is a sample daily allowance as prepared by veterinarian Jean Hofve. The amounts listed are adequate for one day's feeding of a 20- to 35-pound dog. Dachshunds should receive one-third to one-half these amounts. You should adjust the amounts of ingredients and supplements proportionally to your dog's weight. Starches may be decreased in case of digestive problems or for weight loss.

Choose one protein source (meat amounts given in raw weight):
- 1/3 pound boneless chicken breast or thigh, chopped
- 3 large hard-boiled eggs, chopped
- 1/3 pound lean beef, bison, or lamb, ground or minced
- Optional: once a week, substitute 4 oz organic liver for half of any meat source

Choose one starch source:
- 2 cups cooked macaroni
- 3 cups cooked potato, with skin, chopped or mashed
- 2 cups cooked rice
- 2 cups rolled oats, quick, cooked

Supplements:
- Pureed veggie mix, raw or steamed (up to 1 cup)
- 1 tablespoon olive oil, or 1/2 tbsp olive and 1/2 tbsp flaxseed oil
- 400 mg calcium (elemental, as calcium citrate or carbonate) or 1200 mg (approximately $1^1/_2$ tsp) bone meal powder (human grade)
- 1/4 tsp salt substitute (potassium chloride)—give 3 or 4 times a week
- 1 multiple vitamin-mineral supplement (human quality) dose adjusted for weight
- 1 probiotic/digestive enzyme supplement

your dog's health, however, you must resist. That doesn't mean you can't ever give him a bit of your scrambled egg or a piece of cheese or a nibble of your pizza crust. It does mean that you can't give him treats and goodies constantly.

Factor the amount and types of treats you give with what your dog is fed as his regular food. For instance, if you are having a training session every day—especially if you are using clicker training—you will be giving your dog a lot of treats. Cut those treats up into very small pieces, and subtract a bit of kibble or a teaspoon or so of the canned food to compensate.

If you have eggs every morning and you and your Dachshund both enjoy sharing, think about that when you are feeding your dog his regular meal. My dogs get a dog biscuit at night, as well as a smaller one when I leave the house and they stay behind. Some people always give their dog a biscuit when the dog comes in from the yard. When I add cheese to my lunchtime sandwich, both dogs get a bite of

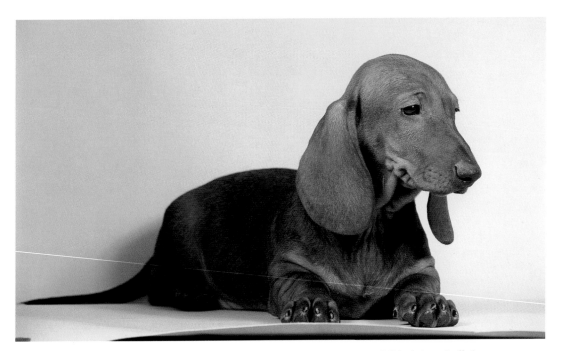

With their typically hearty appetites, pleading eyes, and love of naps, it's easy for Dachshunds to pack on the pounds. Keep an eye on your dog's weight and manage it accordingly.

cheese. Part of the fun of having a dog is getting to sneak them a sliver of turkey or watching them catch popcorn in mid-air.

Sometimes we forget how small our dogs really are and how quickly they can gain weight. Two or three pounds doesn't sound like much to an adult human, but for a Dachshund, that can mean the difference between ideal weight and overweight. A fat dog is not attractive, but more than that, he is not healthy. Extra pounds on your Dachshund can lead to heart problems, breathing problems, and diabetes. It can also add stress to the back and to joints, and that can lead to arthritis, a painful and debilitating condition.

Taking weight off a dog is so much easier than a person. Dogs can't raid the refrigerator in the middle of the night, or reach for a second helping. If your dog is overweight, cut back on treats. This may be enough, but if not, reduce the amount of food at each meal. Try increasing your dog's exercise. Maybe an extra trip around the block will do the trick, or a little more playtime. A good game of hide-and-seek in the house can help burn some calories, and you and your dog will love it.

So many times we equate love with food treats. Our dogs ask for so little and they love goodies so much. Be sensible with treats. Don't kill your dog with kindness.

Getting your Dachshund out for more frequent walks or visits with other dogs can help him get back in shape.

Being Smart About Treats

There are two main things to remember when offering treats: First, no more than 10 percent of your dog's total amount of food should be "people food" or treats. Second, make sure that the treats are appropriate. Treats marketed especially for dogs are fine, and many people foods are okay in small amounts. Others may cause tummy upsets. For instance, at Thanksgiving, a bit of turkey is fine, but stay away from the stuffing, or excessive gravy, which could be too rich. When you're making pies, a spoonful of the canned pumpkin won't hurt, but don't give your Dachshund bites of the finished pie.

Stay away from all chocolates. The theobromine in chocolate can be fatal to dogs and even if it doesn't kill your dog, it can make him sick. The American Animal Hospital Association (AAHA) offers these figures for fatal doses of chocolate: Ten ounces of milk chocolate, or 1/2 to 1 ounce of baking chocolate can kill a small dog; 1 to 1 1/2 pounds of milk chocolate or 2 to 3 ounces of baking chocolate can kill a medium dog.

Liver Treats

People who show their dogs use liver treats as bait to get their dogs to look alert and happy. Whether you show your dog or not, liver makes a wonderful treat. The fast way to make the treats is to put the liver in the microwave, cover it

To gauge your dog's weight, look at him from the top. He should have a bit of an indentation behind the ribs. Feel your Dachshund's sides. You should be able to feel the ribs. If you can't feel the ribs, your Dachshund needs to go on a diet.

with a paper towel, and microwave for three minutes on high. Turn the pieces over, and cook it again for three more minutes on high. The result is a piece of cooked liver that looks a lot like shoe leather. Not attractive to you, but your Dachshund will love it! Feed tiny pieces as a reward.

Another recipe is to put the liver in cold water. Rinse. Add the rinsed liver to a pan of cold water and bring it to a boil. Boil for 20 minutes. Put the liver on a cookie sheet, sprinkle with garlic powder, and bake for 20 to 30 minutes at 300 degrees. This, too, will come out looking shriveled and unappetizing to you—but not to your dog! Keep extra in the freezer.

TEACHING GOOD FOOD MANNERS

Teach good food manners from the time your Dachshund is a puppy. Puppies are so cute it's hard to imagine that we might not want them to be constant beggars when they reach adulthood. Also, what might be manageable when you have just one Dachshund may be annoying if you have two or three or four.

When we got our first dog, I always gave her the milk that was left in my cereal bowl. When we got another dog, I had to divide that milk. With dog number three, I had to actually pour extra milk and make sure each dog got some. It wasn't as cute anymore. The same thing happened with evening snacks.

Foods to be careful of are grapes, raisins, onions, and macadamia nuts. Don't panic if your dog eats a couple of raisins or a grape, or a piece of onion if you accidentally drop one. If your dog finds an entire box of raisins, though, and thinks it is a wonderful snack, check in with your veterinarian. Too many macadamia nuts can cause temporary paralysis, so be careful your Dachshund can't reach that tempting bowl of nibbles.

Small pieces of peeled carrots make excellent snacks for Dachshunds.

Dogs love popcorn, and plain popcorn is a fine treat for dogs. Well, sharing with one dog is far different from sharing with three or four. When we had four dogs, whenever my husband made popcorn, all four would sit and stare until they got their share. Even with only two dogs now, they still demand their popcorn.

To Get, You Have to Give

Right from the beginning, you can use feeding time as a perfect way to get in some training. Start by asking your dog to sit before you put down the bowl of food. Just hold the bowl slightly above and over your dog's head and say, "Sit." As he follows the bowl with his eyes, he should sink into a sit. Immediately praise him and put down the bowl. When he's learned to sit, start teaching a stay.

Give the sit command, and then place the palm of your hand in front of his face and say, "Stay" or "Wait." Put the

Who could resist this face? Regardless of how cute he is, don't feed your Dachshund from your table, and ask him to stay or wait before he gets his meals or treats.

food dish down and immediately say, "Okay," or whatever release word you choose. Gradually increase the time until your Dachshund is waiting until you release him before he starts to eat.

Teaching your Dachshund with food can make the entire process a game, since Dachshunds are always interested in doing whatever will get them the food! If you decide to try clicker training, you'll find that your Dachshund catches on very quickly to the idea of rewards. (More about that in Chapter 6.)

While your puppy is small, teach him that you are allowed to take things away from him and he must not resist or growl or snap. Put the food dish down and wait until your dog starts eating. Pick up the dish, add something tasty, and give the food back. This is letting him know that if you take it away, he'll get something even better. You can do the same thing if he's playing with a toy. Trade him the toy for a cookie.

5 GROOMING

YOUR DACHSHUND

A chapter on grooming your Dachshund needs three different approaches, depending on which coat type your Dachshund has. Let's start with some grooming basics and then discuss each coat type.

GROOMING BASICS

Besides helping to keep your dog and your house tidy, grooming is a good time to check your Dachshund for any injuries or problems. Running your hands over your Dachshund and feeling his legs and feet on a regular basis can help you spot problems while they're still small. You can detect skin problems, or any lumps or bumps, as well as catch any flea or tick invasion. While you're checking your dog over, you can also slide a hand over his ribs. If you can't feel them, it may be time for a doggy diet.

Check your Dachshund's eyes for any discharge or cloudiness. Open his mouth just to make sure all is clear. How are your Dachshund's ears? Any dog with a folded ear can develop ear infections. Catch them early with your grooming once-over. Run your hands around your Dachshund's neck and check for swollen lymph glands.

Grooming Tables

With small dogs like Dachshunds, the grooming process is greatly simplified with a grooming table. You can buy them at pet supply stores or through pet catalogs. I wouldn't be without my grooming table. I bought it originally because I was showing my dogs, but even if I weren't, I really appreciate the table. It puts the dog up on my level and saves both my back and my knees. Also, my dogs are less apt to scoot away from me when they're up on the table. That's not to say they will stay there without help. Use a grooming noose, or keep a firm hold of your dog if you put him on a table. Dachshunds are too small to launch themselves from a table without getting hurt, but that doesn't mean they won't try.

Some people prefer to brush their dogs while they're relaxing and watching television. If that works for you, just leave your brush by your favorite chair, wear old clothes, or cover your lap with a towel, and brush away.

The process and routine of grooming a small dog like a Dachshund are simplified when you use a grooming table.

ALL DOGS NEED GROOMING

If you have a Smooth Dachshund, you may feel that your dog, as a shorthaired dog, will not require much in the way of grooming at all. It is true that Smooth Dachshunds don't have a labor-intensive coat. That short, sleek coat won't mat or get tangles or hold a lot of mud or dirt, but that doesn't mean that a Dachshund doesn't need to be groomed. Don't be fooled by that neat look. Dachshunds shed, and you need to groom them to get rid of dead hair and keep them looking and feeling their best. When your Dachshund is shedding, you'll want to brush him at least every other day to prevent all those tiny little hairs from covering everything in your home. Even when your Dachshund isn't actively shedding, a good weekly brushing will help keep things under control.

Brushing a Smooth

With either a Smooth or a Longhair, brushing is the key to getting all that hair off your Dachshund before it comes off on your sofa. Use a soft bristle brush or a slicker brush on your Smooth and, for loosening the coat when your Smooth is shedding, invest in a rubber currycomb. You can follow the grain of the coat from neck to tail, and it will loosen all the dead fur.

Any disease or soreness or problem of any kind is much easier to treat if it's caught early, and doing a hands-on survey of your Dachshund while you're grooming is a good way to make that early catch.

Brushing a Longhair

With a Longhair, pay attention to behind the ears and elbows, as those areas are usually the first to mat. Comb out that hair, gently working out any snarls or knots with your fingers. If you have a Longhair, eventually his "shawl," the longer hair around his neck, will need to be thinned from time to time, or he will start to look like a lion. It's probably best to have a groomer take care of this.

Some people prefer to brush their dogs while they're sitting down and relaxing.

For Smooth and Longhaired Dachshunds, a soft bristle or slicker brush will loosen and remove the dead fur. Work from the head to the tail.

Brushing a Wirehair

If you have a Wirehair, the grooming is a bit different. Many pet owners use clippers or have a groomer clip the dog. This is faster and easier than stripping, but softens the dog's coat. If you ever plan to show your Wirehair, never, ever use clippers. If you have the time, you can learn to hand-strip your Wirehair, which is a way of plucking out all the dead hair, clearing the way for new growth. Some people also use special stripping knives. Talk to your breeder or a groomer about learning to do this.

Grooming Time as Bonding Time

Don't think of grooming as just a chore to get through as quickly as possible. Grooming is also a good way to bond with your dog. While you're grooming, you are gently restraining your dog, preventing him from hurting either himself or you. This is teaching him in a calm way that you are the boss, the pack leader. Dogs need a leader, and once your Dachshund recognizes you in that role, he's going to be a happier, calmer dog.

Grooming is a wonderful way to sneak in some training, too. Keep those treats handy and reward your Dachshund for standing still, or for lifting a paw, or even lying quietly on his side, although it's hard to imagine a Dachshund lying quietly unless he's asleep!

If you have more than one dog, grooming time provides some one-on-one time for each dog. There's no competition, no race to see who gets into your lap first. It's just you and one dog enjoying each other.

TRIMMING NAILS

Next come the nails. If you've just given a bath, then that's a good time to trim nails, because the water will have softened them up a bit, but if you're just doing a general grooming session that doesn't include a bath, you've got to do the nails as well. Dog nails grow at different rates and, if you walk your dog regularly on pavement, that may be enough to keep the nails worn down, but probably, sooner or later, you will have to cut your dog's nails. Dachshunds are notorious for not liking this process, so you may need help.

Dachshunds are small, but that compact little body is muscular. If you are fortunate enough to have a helper, have her sit in a chair and hold the Dachshund on his back, with the dog's head under the helper's chin. Have her hold on gently but firmly. Take your clippers in one hand and your Dachshund's paw in the other. Again, use a gentle but very firm grip. You don't want your dog pulling away when you are cutting.

Cut the tip of the nail, and try to avoid hitting the quick. The quick is the dark vein running down the middle of the nail. If your Dachshund has black nails, which is likely, this can be tricky. Better to trim just a little at a time than to hit the quick. If you do hit the quick, don't panic. Use a bit of styptic powder to stop the bleeding, give your Dachshund a treat, and continue.

Wirehaired Dachshunds are hand-stripped by professional groomers. Wires also need particular attention paid to their eyebrows and beards.

Another alternative is to find a groomer you like and have her do the nails. I always do that with my male. It may be a coward's way out, but it's better than having nails that could deform your Dachshund's foot and make walking a slippery or painful affair.

Once your dog learns that having his nails clipped is relatively painless and earns him treats, he won't mind the procedure.

Grinding Nails

Another way to trim your Dachshund's nails is to use a grinding tool. My dogs much prefer this to clipping. Start getting your puppy used to the tool by turning it on and gently holding a paw on the tool so he can feel the vibration. Give him a treat. Turn the tool off. After a few days of holding paws against the tool, grasp a paw firmly and grind a nail. Try to do all the nails on one foot, but if your Dachshund starts to fight you, stop for the day and try again the next day. It shouldn't take long before your dog accepts the grinder. With one of my dogs, I still just do one foot, then stop, give a treat and a hug, then do the next foot, and so on.

Removing Sticky Stuff

If your Dachshund gets something sticky in his coat, like gum, tree sap, or road tar, use an ice cube to freeze it. If the substance is brittle, it will come out of the coat more easily. Or, try peanut butter on the gooey stuff. I like both these ideas for anything on the face.

If there's something sticky on the body, hairspray soaked onto the spot may work, or try a cotton ball soaked with nail polish remover. Just be careful with both of these products as they may irritate your Dachshund's skin.

This Dachshund's nails are short and neat.

MINDING THE EARS

Check your Dachshund's ears on a regular basis. Doing so helps you catch any problems while they're still small. The inside of the ear should be pink, not red. You can find special ear cleaner at pet supply shops and at most veterinarian's offices. Check the label to see if the product contains alcohol, which can dry out and irritate your Dachshund's ears and make them itch. Squirt some cleaner on a cotton ball, and gently clean the inside flap of your dog's ears. Also, gently clean around the outer ear. Don't ever poke into the ear canal. If you feel some deep cleaning is needed or that

All Dachshunds need to have the insides of their ears cleaned regularly.

your Dachshund might have a serious infection, or ear mites, make an appointment with your veterinarian.

BATH TIME
Preparation Is Key

If it's time for a bath, get everything ready before you get your dog. There's no way he's going to wait patiently in one spot while you scurry around looking for your supplies. In fact, you may want to get a small bucket and keep all the equipment for bathing in one spot.

First, think about where you're going to bathe your Dachshund. If you have a miniature, your kitchen sink may work if you don't mind the thought of washing your dog there. If you have a utility tub in your laundry room or basement, that might work as well. Both of these places have the advantage over your bathtub of being at counter height. This will save both your back and your knees. If your kitchen faucet has a spray attachment, this is even better.

If you don't want to use a sink, then it will have to be the bathtub. You can buy a shower-like attachment for the bathtub faucet, which will make wetting down your dog and rinsing him much easier, or you can use a pitcher to pour water over your Dachshund. I like spray or shower attachments because I think the water gets right down to the skin and I know that all the soap residue has been removed.

Wherever you choose to give the bath, make sure there's a nonslip surface for your Dachshund. If your dog doesn't feel secure, he's more likely to struggle and more likely to injure himself. If you've selected the bathtub, get yourself a foam pad or a thick towel to kneel on. Get lots of towels for your dog. Change into clothing that you don't care about; something that can get soaking wet, because you will get wet, especially if your Dachshund decides to shake—and believe me, he will.

If you'd like to use a vinegar rinse, have that ready as well. Apple cider vinegar helps clear any soap residue from the coat and smells nice. For Dachshunds, use about 1/4 cup to every 4 cups of water. Be very careful not to get any soap or vinegar in your Dachshund's eyes. Some groomers add a drop of mineral oil to the eyes to help protect against soap, but others feel this just helps spread the soap. I've never used anything in my dog's eyes, but I am careful with soap. I never

It's best not to use shampoo formulated for people; a special dog shampoo will have the right pH balance for your dog and won't dry or irritate his skin.

shampoo my dog's face. I just gently wipe the face with a damp cloth.

Some people put a cotton ball in each of the dog's ears to prevent soap and water from getting in. It's been my experience that the dog will keep shaking his head until the cotton comes out, so I never bother with the cotton, I just use care. Generally, I just clean the face and ears separately and shampoo from the head back.

If you are going to clean ears at this time, make sure you've got those cleaning supplies at hand, as well as your shampoo and towels. Once you've got your dog, close the door to the room where you're giving the bath. If you have more than one dog, they're going to be a distraction otherwise and, if you're giving the bath in the bathroom and your Dachshund manages to escape from the tub, you don't want water and suds all over the house.

A cup of oatmeal and a cup of baking soda mixed into a quart of warm water can make a soothing rinse if your Dachshund is suffering from any kind of dermatitis.

It's Bath Time!

With supplies at hand and your dog in the room, you're ready to bathe. Before I put my dog in a tub or sink, I run the water and get it the right temperature. I don't want to have to hold a squirming dog and try to adjust the water, and I don't want to risk the water being too hot. So, adjust the water, and then put the dog in the tub. Wet the dog thoroughly with either a sprayer or with a container. Add some shampoo and work up a lather. The first application

With all your supplies at hand, adjust the water temperature and then put your Dachshund in the tub.

Be sure to have clean, dry towels at the ready so you can rub down and dry off your Dachshund after his bath.

may not suds up much, but that's okay. It is cutting the dirt and oil. Rinse. Lather again. Don't neglect the feet. Rinse again. Keep rinsing until the water runs clear. Make sure you get all the soap off. Pay attention to behind the elbows and on the stomach. And remember to rinse those tootsies.

Try to wrap a towel around your dog before he comes out of the tub. Always lift the dog out; don't let him try to scramble out on his own. He could easily get hurt. Towel your dog as dry as possible. This will take more than one towel, so be prepared. In warm weather, this may be enough. If you want to use a hair dryer on your longhair either use a special dog hair dryer, or, if you're using your own dryer, put it on its lowest setting. Dogs are very sensitive, and a setting that is fine for a human is too hot for a dog. If your dryer has an air-only setting, that's even better.

If you're doing the bath at home, don't let your dog outside immediately following the bath. Nine times out of ten a dog will roll in the grass, or worse, the nearest patch of dirt. After all your hard work, enjoy it awhile before you let your dog get dirty again.

CARING FOR YOUR DOG'S TEETH

Dachshund puppies are like all puppies everywhere: they love to chew. Chewing feels good when puppies are teething, and, depending on what they chew, it also helps keep their teeth clean and their gums healthy. Chewing is also one of the ways puppies learn about their world. Human toddlers and puppies are alike in that they will try to put anything and everything into their mouths.

Make sure you rinse your Dachshund repeatedly to remove all the soapy residue from the shampoo.

Appropriate Chew Toys

It's your job to make sure that what they chew on is safe. Also, if you don't want your chair rungs destroyed, or holes in your rug, or your kitchen linoleum pulled up, you should supply your puppy with approved chew toys.

If your puppy is teething, cold things will feel good on his sore gums. Wet a washcloth (one you are willing to sacrifice to sharp teeth), put it in a plastic bag, and freeze it. When it's frozen, take it out of the bag and let your puppy chew on it. An ice cube may also make a good teething toy. Keeping nylon bones in the freezer in between chewing sessions will make them more attractive, too. Raw carrots and whole apples make good, safe chew toys as well.

Hard, crunchy dog biscuits are helpful, as are nylon bones and rawhide bones or strips.

Nylon vs. Rawhide

The nylon bones get rough ends as they are chewed, acting like a toothbrush, and any small bits of nylon that may be ingested pass harmlessly through the system. Rawhide bones are also good, but require more supervision. Some dogs experience no trouble with rawhide, but other dogs tend to chew off large chunks and swallow them whole. These swallowed chunks can lead to intestinal blockage or stomach upset. Rawhide strips are more likely to cause this kind of a problem than a rawhide bone, but both can cause

Hard nylon bones make excellent chews for Dachshunds. The nubs on this one also stimulate the gums.

problems. The rawhide form least likely to cause problems is the pressed rawhide bone, which is made up of tiny shavings of rawhide that are molded into a bone shape. This eliminates the worry of the dog biting off and swallowing large, indigestible chunks.

Rawhide doesn't last as long as nylon bones, either. While a nylon bone may seem more expensive, it will be cheaper in the long run. Even small dogs like Dachshunds can demolish large rawhide bones quickly. Also, if you have more than one dog, they are more apt to get into a fight over the rawhide than they are over the nylon bones. To assess the best nylon bone for your Dachshund, visit the Nylabone web site at www.nylabone.com.

Bones

Real bones require the most supervision of all. While a large knucklebone is probably safe for your Dachshund to chew on, many bones can splinter, or will have sharp points that can harm your dog. Swallowing bone shards can lead to serious problems if those pieces should pierce the intestines. Even with smooth bones, such as beef marrow bones, if your dog is an aggressive chewer, he can end up with a large mass of indigestible bone in his stomach, which can lead to vomiting, or even a blockage in the intestine. Real bones, if given at all, should be fed outside. They are usually too messy to allow the dog to gnaw on your carpeting.

Rope toys can be very effective at cleaning your dog's teeth, but again, supervise your dog while he plays with this kind of a toy. Dachshunds, even puppies, can totally destroy a toy in very little time, and you don't want your dog to swallow the strings, which could cause serious intestinal damage.

Brushing the Teeth

Besides providing appropriate chew toys for your dog, you can also help with his dental health by brushing his teeth regularly. Dental care is as important in dogs as it is in people, and starting young will help to protect your dog's health. Although dogs are not as susceptible to tooth decay as humans, they do develop plaque, which, if not removed, hardens to tartar. Tartar, in turn, can cause abscesses, and the bacteria from those abscesses can circulate in the system and lead to pneumonia or heart, liver, or kidney problems.

If you do give your Dachshund a real bone to enjoy in the yard, make sure that you discard it after a day or two. Any longer than that and it will get dry and hard and can cause as much damage as a cooked bone.

There are toothbrushes and toothpaste made specially for dogs, making proper oral hygiene easier than ever.

There are special brushes for brushing your dog's teeth, as well as smaller plastic "brushes" that fit over your finger. Or, you can wrap a piece of gauze around your finger and use that to go over the dog's teeth and gently rub the gums. Most veterinarians and pet supply stores also have special pastes for brushing your dog's teeth. These pastes come in flavors like chicken or liver. If you use a paste, make sure it is a paste made especially for dogs; never use human toothpaste on your dog.

Bad Breath

Your dog's breath will never smell like a bouquet of spring flowers, but it shouldn't make you gag, either. If you notice that your Dachshund's breath is really bad, check out his mouth. Make sure there are no chunks of food or bone stuck anywhere. Take a look at his teeth at the same time. Are they clean, or covered with plaque?

If you think the cause of the odor is just temporary because of something your dog may have eaten, a few chlorophyll tablets might be just the thing, or try giving your dog a rawhide or nylon or real bone to chew, to help scrape off some of the plaque. The occasional piece of raw carrot will help do the same thing.

If you're brushing your Dachshund's teeth regularly, but there's still bad breath, it may be time for a professional cleaning.

Your veterinarian may recommend a professional cleaning procedure under anesthesia to thoroughly cleanse and polish your dog's teeth.

When you're at your veterinarian's office for the cleaning, ask for recommendations to prevent bad breath. Your veterinarian may suggest switching from a soft food to a hard kibble. He may want to schedule your Dachshund for regular cleanings. Not all dogs need frequent cleanings, but some do.

Whatever you think may be the cause of doggy bad breath, don't ignore it. Bad breath may be an indication of something more serious. Instead of just trying to avoid your dog's breath, see if you can identify any particular smell. A sweet, fruity smell could mean your dog has diabetes, especially if he is drinking or urinating more than usual and is losing weight. If his breath smells like urine, he might have a kidney disease. A foul odor that's accompanied by vomiting, loss of appetite, swelling of the abdomen, or yellowing of the eyes or gums could indicate a liver disorder.

Professional Cleanings

Your veterinarian may at some time in your dog's life recommend a professional cleaning for your dog's teeth. This involves anesthetizing your dog. While your dog is asleep, the veterinarian or technician removes any tartar buildup, then cleans and polishes your dog's teeth, much like your dentist cleans your own teeth. If any cracked or broken teeth are found, they will be removed at the same time. If there are any abscesses, or if there is infection anywhere in the gum, your dog will probably be put on an antibiotic.

Dental care is easily overlooked, but statistics show that 75 percent of all dogs have some kind of periodontal problem by the time they are four years old. So, include your Dachshund's mouth and teeth in every health check.

If your dog is older, the veterinarian may also recommend blood tests before the cleaning to make sure the dog can safely handle the anesthesia. This safe guard is well worth it, and, with older dogs, may help your veterinarian detect other health problems as well.

Not all dogs are alike, of course. Some dogs may need their teeth cleaned every six months; some may go their entire lives without needing a professional cleaning. Have your veterinarian check your dog's teeth at least once a year and, if you notice that your Dachshund's breath smells more than his normal "dog breath," or if he is drooling, or pawing at his mouth, or is having trouble eating hard food and no longer wants to chew on toys or bones, make an appointment with your veterinarian.

TRAINING AND BEHAVIOR
O F   Y O U R   D A C H S H U N D

Many people think small dogs don't need any training, and it's true, small dogs can be easily scooped up if they're getting into trouble. Even a standard Dachshund can be picked up with a bit of effort, but you and your Dachshund will both be happier if he has some training. Your Dachshund will know there are limits, and he will respect you as the one who has set those limits.

All dogs, even small dogs, are pack animals. They are social and need to be part of a group, or a pack. Just two dogs can be a pack. Or, your dog's pack may be you and your family. Every pack needs a leader and, if there is no leader, your dog will try to fill the position. He may not even really want to be the leader, but someone needs to lead, and he'll feel he has to do it if no one else does.

ARE YOU A FAIR LEADER?

So, even with a small dog, you need to be the leader of the pack. You do this by being firm, fair, and consistent. You don't do it by yelling or screaming. You set the rules, not the dog. This doesn't mean that you don't have lots of cuddle time and together time, but it does mean that you pick those times. Even small dogs can be possessive. It's just fine to allow your Dachshund to join you on the couch or on your bed, but make it at your invitation, not whenever he feels like it. Decide on a command. It doesn't have to be fancy. Most likely, just patting the seat or the bed beside you will be enough of an invitation. After awhile, tell him, "Off," and help him to the floor. If your bed or couch is high, helping him is always a good idea so your Dachshund doesn't hurt himself. You might even want to make a ramp or a small set of stairs.

WHAT DO YOU WANT YOUR DACHSHUND TO DO?

There are two levels of training—household manners and formal training—and even if you have no interest in formal training, all dogs should exhibit good household manners. Household manners can vary with the household, but housetraining is pretty basic. Other "manners" training might include not jumping on the furniture, no begging at the table, no jumping up on people, and no excessive barking. You might also want to teach your Dachshund to leave the cat or some other household pet alone.

Establishing Rules

Waiting to be fed, and not charging out the door ahead of you when you're going for a walk are two more examples of household manners. Again, you are the pack leader. The leader always goes first. Make your Dachshund sit at the door on your way for a walk. Step through the door first, then call your dog through. Do this when feeding, as well. Have your Dachshund wait until you put the food dish down. Take the dish away occasionally, and then give it back. You are the leader and should be able to do this at any time.

In fact, all the human members of your family should be above your Dachshund in pack rank. Your Dachshund will learn quickly what he should and shouldn't do as long as you are consistent and patient. Part of the consistency means that the entire family must be part of the training team. It does no good for Mom to try to teach the dog not to jump up if Dad and the kids encourage the dog to jump up, or if they pet and praise him when he does. That's sending a mixed message.

The same goes for housetraining. I once heard about a puppy who was taking a long time to understand the concept of going outdoors. Finally, someone in the family realized that, with all the different doors and sliding doors in

If your Dachshund doesn't understand what you want him to do, it will be hard for him to comply.

their house, family members were going in and out whichever door was handiest. The puppy never got a sense of which door he should go to when he needed to go out. And there was no designated area outside that was his spot. Once everyone agreed on one door and one area of the yard, the puppy quickly learned the routine.

Right from the beginning, agree on what will be allowed and what won't. There's nothing nicer than snuggling with your Dachshund on the couch, but if the family rule is no dogs on the furniture, then make sure no one allows the dog on the couch, ever, not even as a cute little puppy. The same goes for sleeping on beds. And, if you don't want your little chowhound looking pathetic and begging for some popcorn every time you have a snack, then don't feed him a handful while you're watching a video. Ever.

In the wild, predators develop habits that help them to find food in the most efficient way possible. If a wolf catches a rabbit in a particular spot, he's likely to continue to visit that spot, as this may be a regular path for rabbits.

It's a lot harder to break a dog of a habit like begging than it is to start the habit, so think carefully about what you will and will not accept, and make sure everyone in the family knows and follows the rules.

SOCIALIZING YOUR DACHSHUND

Dachshunds are by nature friendly and loving, but it's up to you to encourage those traits. A puppy raised in isolation may be shy and fearful. Socialization is an important part of your commitment to your dog.

Start from the day your puppy comes home. Put his crate in a part of the house that sees a lot of activity, like the kitchen or the family room. Let him get used to the sounds of dinner being prepared, the phone ringing, the teakettle whistling. Let him hear the television or a radio. Have family and friends pet and play with the puppy. Introduce him to different toys and to different surfaces underfoot. Carpeting, tile, a piece of plastic, or wood—all of these things help to build confidence in your puppy.

Once your puppy has all his shots, take him for walks around the neighborhood. Encourage people to gently pet your puppy. If you don't have children, find some. Children, with their sudden movements and high-pitched voices, may frighten a dog, and a frightened dog may bite. I made sure I took my male to places where there were children. I supervised closely, but I encouraged children to pet him and play with him.

With people you trust or in a class situation, it's great to be able to let your Dachshund socialize with other dogs.

Don't let children grab your Dachshund around the middle and lift. It's not good for your Dachshund's back, and, it may startle him and cause him to snap. In that position, the child's face is right next to the dog's muzzle. Children should be encouraged to pet your dog, but never to tightly hug or lift your dog.

Besides neighborhood children, I took my dog to Girl Scout meetings. While teaching the scouts how to approach a strange dog, how to pet a dog, and how to give a dog a treat, I was also teaching my dog that strangers were nothing to be afraid of and might even have goodies.

Take your Dachshund with you when you run errands. Carry him into the bank. Sit on a bench at a shopping mall. Dachshunds are so cute that people are going to want to pet your dog. Let them. Carry extra treats and ask some of the people to give the treats to your dog.

If there are mostly women in your house or in your circle of friends, make an effort to find men to pet and play with your Dachshund. Find big men with beards. Find people wearing hats and glasses. Take your Dachshund to a playground and let him see bicycles and skateboards. If there's a dog park in your neighborhood, even if you don't feel you can let your dog loose in the park, visit the park and get your Dachshund used to seeing other dogs. If you have a friend or neighbor with a friendly dog, introduce the dogs.

If the dog is much bigger than your Dachshund, be

If there are no dog parks and no neighborhood dogs who are good candidates as playmates, consider enrolling in a puppy kindergarten class or an obedience class so that your Dachshund can get used to being around other dogs.

careful. A big dog could accidentally hurt your Dachshund in play, or your Dachshund could feel threatened by a larger dog looming over him and he could snap or bite. It's good for your dog to have other dogs as friends, but make the introductions on neutral ground, keep the dogs leashed, and make the introduction slowly.

Expose your dog to as many different sights and sounds as you can when he is young, and you should end up with a happy, outgoing, friendly dog.

A CRATE CAN BE GREAT

Along with your puppy's health record, a supply of food, and a toy or two, your breeder may also have talked to you about a crate for your puppy. A crate, like any tool, can be abused; however, when used correctly, it can make day-to-day living with your Dachshund much more pleasant for everyone. If your puppy came with a crate, or your breeder started crate training, then you're a step ahead. Otherwise, go get a crate now. No, it is not a cage, and no, it is not cruel. Dogs are den animals. Think of all the dogs you've seen resting under a table or a chair. They appreciate the security of a small, dark space. People see bars; dogs see security.

If you have a multi-dog household, or there's a lot of activity in your home, you'll find that your dog will seek out his crate on his own for an afternoon nap. If you're having a party, or the grandkids are spending the day, pop your Dachshund in his crate to keep him safe or allow him to rest.

Another good reason to have a crate for a puppy is that when you are unable to watch him, you know he will be safe. Puppies check out their world by putting everything in their mouths. That can include the fringe on your oriental rug, the rungs of the antique chair, and electrical cords. While you might be very annoyed at losing the fringe or seeing teeth marks on the chair, if your puppy chews through an electric cord, you're going to lose your puppy.

Travel is another very good reason to have a crate. For one thing, you don't want your Dachshund traveling loose in the car. A crate will keep him safe and he won't be climbing into the driver's lap and distracting him. Also, travel can be stressful. If your Dachshund has his own safe crate at the end of the trip, that will help keep him calmer. Motels may more readily accept you and your dog if they know the dog will be crated and not left alone to chew on the bedspread. Even the best-trained dogs may, from anxiety, have an accident. A crate will prevent it from being on the motel room carpet.

Your own relatives and friends may also appreciate the crate. If you're visiting and are taking the dog, a crate will reassure your loved ones that their possessions will be the same when you leave as they were when you arrived.

One of the best tools for housetraining is your crate. Dogs don't like to soil their own bed. Given a chance, and within a reasonable time frame, a puppy will learn to hold it until he is taken to an appropriate spot. The other advantage to a crate is that it has a small, easy-to-clean surface, so if the

Crate training has multiple benefits. It not only assists in housetraining, but it provides a safe den or carrier for quiet time or traveling.

puppy does have an accident in the crate, it is easier to clean than the rug, and causes less damage (and anger).

Without a crate, your Dachshund puppy may opt to use the furniture for the frequent naps he needs.

Crate Limits

Until your Dachshund is housetrained and about a year old, when you leave the house for work or shopping, pop him in his crate. Make sure he has water and maybe a toy or two. This does not mean put your Dachshund in a crate at 8 a.m. and leave him until you get home at 6 p.m. A crate is a useful training tool and a safe haven for your dog, but it is not a substitute for training, or for attention.

The rule for puppies is that they can be crated for their age in months, plus one. So, if your puppy is two months old, three hours is the limit. The other rule is, no longer than four hours for any dog, puppy or adult. If there's no family member who can give the dog a break after four hours, see if there's a neighbor who can help out, turn a laundry room or bathroom into a place for your Dachshund during the day, or hire a professional pet-walking service.

There will be exceptions, of course. If you're visiting relatives and are going out for the afternoon, your adult Dachshund will not suffer if he's crated for six hours. Just make this kind of crating the exception rather than the rule. And, before you crate your Dachshund for an extended period of time, make sure he's had a chance to relieve himself.

You don't want your puppy or dog to learn that whining or crying is what opens the crate door to let him out. If your dog is upset in the crate, make no noise yourself until he is quiet. The second he stops protesting, open the door and praise him. Gradually increase the amount of time in the crate.

Crate Training Your Puppy

If you have a puppy, crate training should not be difficult at all. To begin, make the crate a comfortable, enjoyable place. Put in lots of towels, a toy, and water. I like the toy to be a cuddly stuffed toy for puppies, as I think it reminds them of their littermates. Think about a bowl that clamps to the side of the crate, or a water bottle, so the puppy won't tip the bowl over.

To introduce your puppy to the crate, allow him to investigate with the door open. Toss a small treat into the crate. When he follows, praise him. Let him come out for another small treat. Next time, toss the treat in the crate and when he goes to get it, close the door for about 30 seconds. Praise him and repeat again, this time for about 30 seconds longer. This is a great way to build his tolerance and get him used to being in his crate in a gradual way.

Most puppies readily accept the crate. Sometimes they'll cry a bit at night, especially the first two or three nights. Harden your heart, grit your teeth, and don't take him out. If you've made sure that he's relieved himself and you know he's warm and dry, just try to listen to those heart-breaking sounds without giving in. He'll get used to it, honest.

If you have more than one crate, or can easily shift your crate, let your dog sleep in the bedroom with you. It may make falling asleep a bit more difficult for those first few nights, but it will give your dog more time with you, even if you're asleep. It's like eight hours of quality time for your dog, with no effort on your part. Another advantage is that you can hear your puppy if he whines and needs to go out in the middle of the night.

Crate Training an Older Dog

If you've brought home an older dog who's never had a crate, it's still worthwhile to crate train him, but it will be more of a project. Start by putting the crate in a central place like the kitchen or family room. Leave the door open. Feed

Crate Quirks

Sometimes there will be a dog who just can't adjust to a crate, and some dogs develop their own little quirks. I've had three dogs who slept in their crates each night, but insisted that the door be left open. One dog always started out sleeping under the bed and then moved to her crate. My male won't settle down unless he's in his closed crate, but my girl prefers the freedom to roam around a bit at night. Train your dogs to accept the crate, but with time, you'll know what variations might be called for.

your dog in the crate, still leaving the door open. During the day, occasionally throw a tasty treat into the crate. If your dog happens to go into the crate on his own, praise and treat him. If you have a clicker, you can click and treat. After three or four days, close the door while your Dachshund is eating. Open it and let him out as soon as he's finished eating. Put a longer-lasting treat, like a rawhide or a carrot in the crate, and shut the door.

At odd times during the day, put him in the crate, shut the door, and leave him. Keep the time short, but don't ever let him out when he's barking. Wait until he is silent, and then open the door. You don't want to reward the barking. Within a couple of weeks, your dog should have accepted the crate as his den.

Crates can be fairly expensive, but they last forever, so make the investment. First you'll have to decide which kind of crate you want. For shows, or traveling, I prefer the hard-sided crates as they offer better protection. The Nylabone Fold-Away Den & Carrier is ideal for owners who need a crate they can carry to different places and fold quickly to store or move. For a permanent spot at home, I like wire crates because they provide more ventilation, especially in the summer. To make it more den-like, I cover the crate with

When you need to secure your dog outside for a short time (under your supervision), you may choose to use a wire exercise pen rather than a more enclosed crate.

a towel. Then, in the summer, it's easy to flip the sides up to allow for more air.

As wonderful as crates are for training, for security, and for safety, remember, they are not a substitute for training or for companionship. If you don't have the time to spend exercising and playing and cuddling with a Dachshund, you better think about getting a goldfish.

SUCCESSFUL HOUSETRAINING

Along with the crate training, you'll want to train your puppy to eliminate outdoors. Many people will tell you that Dachshunds are hard to housetrain, but part of that is based on the history of hunting dogs. Hunting dogs were selected for their ability to trail and, in the case of Dachshunds, to be fearless in the face of prey. They were not necessarily selected because they were easy to train. A Dachshund can be a bit stubborn on certain issues. Dachshunds can definitely be housetrained, but it's up to you to be consistent and to have a schedule.

There is more than one way to housetrain a puppy, but no matter what the method used, the key to success is consistency on your part, and a schedule that a young puppy can reasonably meet. No matter what method you use, when you take your puppy out, choose a word or phrase that will be your puppy's cue to "go." It could be "hurry up," or "go potty" or anything at all. Once your dog is housetrained, this phrase can come in handy. If you're going somewhere for a few hours, take your dog out, say the command phrase and your dog should "go." Then you can leave him alone at home without worrying about accidents.

When you take your puppy out, take him out on a lead. You want to be able to direct him to the right spot. Puppies are fast and curious, which means they can get over and under obstacles, and they will. If you're dressed for work, you won't want to have to crawl in the dirt under a bush, and if it's 2 a.m. and you're in your nightgown, your puppy may appreciate a game of tag, but you probably won't.

Housetraining With a Crate

First, let's discuss housetraining with a crate. Take the puppy out first thing in the morning. Open the crate, remove the puppy, and head for the yard. Do not open the

Never, ever punish your puppy for mistakes. If you catch him in the act, scoop him up with his tail between his thighs to prevent further spillage, and rush him outside. Praise him when he goes in the right place. Yelling at him after the fact does no good at all. Housetraining takes patience and observation and consistency on your part. Also, never rub your dog's nose in his mistake. This will only teach him that he needs to hide his "mistake" from you.

crate and coax the puppy to follow you through the house to the yard. The puppy is probably not going to make it that far. Carry him, so that he goes in the yard, in the spot you've chosen. The fewer mistakes that are made in the house, the faster the housetraining will be.

Praise your puppy when he goes in the right spot. Then take him in the house for breakfast, both his and yours. Keep him crated while you eat just in case. Take him back out 20 to 30 minutes after he's eaten. Give him some playtime before everyone leaves for school or work. Take him out one more time. Put him back in his crate for no more than four hours. If you can't get home for lunch, see if there's a neighbor who can help. Take the puppy out immediately. There should also be another meal, some playtime and another trip out, and then back in the crate.

If you have children, this means that in another two or three hours someone will be home for another trip out and more play time. Make sure everyone understands the importance of getting the puppy outdoors when he needs to relieve himself. Puppies typically sniff and circle but they are also very quick, and, with Dachshund puppies, sometimes it's hard to tell if they're squatting or not.

After dinner, it's out again, and another play session. Then, because puppies, like babies, need lots of sleep, your puppy may sleep during the evening while you're watching television. Take him out one last time at about 11 p.m. If he's kept warm all night, he should make it until you are up at 6 a.m. to start the day. Puppies are a lot like people in that regard. If your puppy gets cold in the night, he'll wake up and if he wakes up, he'll have to go. Having a crate in the bedroom means that not only does the puppy get to be with you, but, if he wakes up and cries to go out, you'll hear him right away.

Cleaning Up the Messes

Another thing to think about is what kind of cleaning product you use to clean up after your puppy. Never use any cleaning product that contains ammonia. Puppies tend to return to whatever spot they've used before. Scent tells them they've come to the right place. Urine contains ammonia, so if you clean with an ammonia-based cleaner, that residue will tell the puppy he's in the right place. Because this is important, use a commercially prepared enzyme cleaner that removes both the stain and the odor of urine. There are many available to choose from.

Paper Training

Suppose you have no neighbors or children and can't get away regularly for the mid-day walk. In this case, you should consider paper training. Choose a room for confining the puppy. It could be your kitchen, bathroom, or laundry room. If the room is too large to easily cover the floor with newspapers, you can block off a section. Put the puppy's crate and toys and water bowl in the chosen area.

When you are home, try to follow the schedule as discussed under using the crate. Take the puppy out after naps, after meals, and after playtime. When unattended, place the puppy in the papered area. When you clean up, remove the top layers of paper and replace with fresh ones. After a week or so, reduce the area covered by paper. If the puppy successfully uses the paper and not the uncovered floor, reduce the area even further. Continue until all the papers have been picked up.

A relatively new approach is puppy litter. Just like a cat, you can teach your dog to use a litter pan filled with special litter. Litter may be just the thing as an interim step, like the newspapers, or, if you live in an apartment, this may be your permanent solution. Remember, whatever method you use, be patient and be consistent.

Time and Patience

Housetraining may take until the puppy is 12 to 16 weeks old, or possibly longer, depending on the puppy, but it's not something that can be rushed. Also, even if your puppy seems reliable at 16 weeks, there may be lapses. If someone is home with the puppy, he can probably have the run of the house, but if you're going out, don't leave the puppy loose. Take the precaution of putting him in his crate, or in a safe room. Besides the possibility of an accident, puppies love to chew. Don't give him the chance to chew the fringe of the Oriental rug, or the rung of a chair, or, worse yet, an electrical cord.

LEASH TRAINING

The next thing you want to think about after housetraining, or even as part of housetraining, is leash

The APDT

The Association of Pet Dog Trainers (APDT) certifies trainers, and its members consistently use positive-based methods. Find an APDT trainer near you through their web site, www.apdt.com.

training. You may not care about having your Dachshund in a perfect heel position, but it's a good idea to teach him to walk on a lead. Even with a fenced yard, you may want to show off your darling with a walk around the block, and there will certainly be trips to the veterinarian.

First, get your puppy used to the lead. Fasten a light lead to his collar and let him drag it along. Do this only when you're supervising. You don't want the lead to snag on something. Then pick up the end of the lead.

Encourage your puppy to follow you by using a happy voice and treats. If your puppy stops, or veers off in another direction, encourage him to return to you. Do not tug, pull, or yank at him. When your Dachshund understands that the lead is connecting the two of you, try short walks. If your Dachshund pulls, stop walking. He'll likely turn around and look at you, wondering why you're not following. When the

There are many kinds of leashes on the market that serve different purposes. Choose one that's practical and comfortable as well as stylish.

Training and Behavior of Your Dachshund 99

Never, ever put a training collar on your dog and then leave your dog unattended. If the ring catches on something, your dog could choke to death.

lead is slack, start walking again. If he pulls again, repeat the process. Don't yell, don't scream, and don't yank.

With or without a clicker, you can use treats to convince your Dachshund that walking next to you—or at least close enough to keep the lead slack—is a good idea. I keep my dog interested by randomly saying her name and throwing her a treat. Besides keeping her close, this is a good way to get her attention if there are distractions. If I see another person approaching walking a dog, I can say her name and offer a treat, and she is focusing on me instead of wanting to bark at the other dog.

Leash Styles

There are many different kinds of collars and leads on the market. I prefer a soft, thin leather lead, but sometimes these are hard to find. Most pet supply stores will have cotton or nylon leads that work well. Six feet is a good length. Stay away from chain leads. You don't need one to control your Dachshund and, if you're holding it and your Dachshund suddenly dashes after a chipmunk, the chain can tear the skin on your hand.

If you have a park to walk in, you may want to get a retractable lead to allow your Dachshund a bit more freedom. I find them annoying and awkward, but many people love them.

The thing to keep in mind is that most retractable leads allow your dog from 15 to 25 feet of roaming room. Remember to bring your dog back to your side if other people or dogs are approaching. Not every person wants to say hello to your dog and not every approaching dog will be friendly. Your own dog may not be friendly. This is sometimes very hard for people to understand. Just because one dog loves everyone, including other dogs, doesn't mean the reverse is true. Keep your Dachshund under control and away from other dogs, especially if the other dog walker indicates that his dog is not friendly.

What is your lead attached to? Some leads come with a built-in collar. Just slip the loop over your dog's head and go. While these are great for just getting your Dachshund from the house to the car, I don't like them for actual walks. For one thing, when they're loose, the loop can open to a size where a flip of the head sets your Dachshund free. If I'm using a one-piece collar and lead, I prefer the "show lead" type. These open up to easily slip over the dog's head, then a little sliding clip or bead tightens the collar so it fits snugly, but doesn't continue to tighten.

Trainers and owners today recognize that positive, reward-based training methods are the most effective and pleasant.

Choosing a Collar

A flat nylon or leather buckle collar will work well on your Dachshund. You really shouldn't need much more with a Dachshund, but you should know what else there is.

Let's start with the training collar. This may be of chain or nylon, and it consists of a ring that slides freely up and down the collar, and a ring that fastens to the lead. To correctly put this on your Dachshund, form the letter "P" with the collar. The straight part of the letter should be parallel to the ground, with the loop hanging free. If your Dachshund is on your left, slide the loop over his head. This allows the collar to hang loosely until you take up the slack with the lead.

Another kind of collar is the martingale, which is made of two loops. One loop runs through the two rings of the first loop. This is easy to slip over your dog's head, and the top loop means you can draw the bottom loop closed so that it stays around your Dachshund's throat, but it can only be pulled closed so far. There's no danger of your Dachshund choking. If your Dachshund isn't wearing a collar all the time, this is a good type for taking walks because it is so easy

Keep your training sessions short and happy. Three or four short sessions of 5 minutes is more effective than one session of 20 minutes, especially with a puppy.

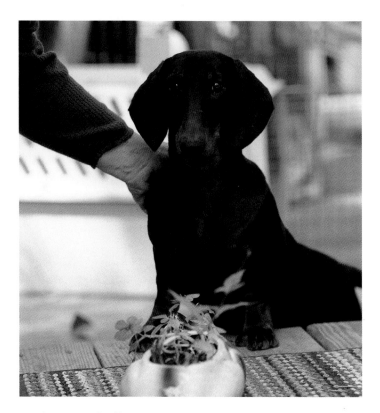

Once your Dachshund has learned what sit means, reinforce the learning by asking him to do it many times during the day.

to slip on and off.

Pinch collars have small prongs that point in and, when pulled tight, they pinch your dog's neck. With large breeds, these collars can be a useful training tool, but there shouldn't be any reason to use one with a Dachshund.

Consider a Harness

Possibly you won't want a collar at all, but will opt for a harness. A harness is a good choice if you're going to use some kind of seat belt system in your car instead of a crate. Many of these devices work better with a harness. When you're taking a walk, you'll have less control with a harness. It's all too easy for your dog to lean into the harness and pull, as there's nothing around his throat to slow him down. With a determined Dachshund who has found a scent to follow, and has decided not to listen to you, a harness may not be a good thing.

If you do decide on a harness, make sure that you buy the right size. Too loose or too tight and it may rub and cause sores. Also, if you buy a harness before your Dachshund is full grown, make sure it's adjustable, or realize that you'll need to buy another one as your dog grows. Either way, with collars and harnesses, keep an eye on the size. What fits your puppy will not work for your dog.

Another alternative is the head halter, which fits over your dog's head much like a horse's halter. This eliminates any choking or harm to your dog's throat, but some people feel that, used incorrectly, a head halter may cause disc damage to the neck and spine. Talk to your breeder, your other Dachshund-owning friends, and your veterinarian.

BASIC OBEDIENCE TRAINING

Training used to mean no treats, a training collar, a lead, and frequently pushing or pulling your dog into the position desired. Working this way, dogs learned to sit, stay down and many other things. But did they enjoy it? Did they ever understand about learning? Since we can't ask the dogs, we'll never know. As training moves away from this method, it's important to remember that, used correctly, this method was not cruel. A dog was never corrected until he had learned a command, and, when he did obey, there was lavish praise, typically in a high, happy voice.

Today, most training methods focus more on food rewards. It seems to be more fun for both the dogs and the people, and certainly, with clicker training, dogs seem to understand the process of learning.

While it is not a good idea to start formal training, or even puppy classes, until your dog has had all his vaccinations, you can start some simple training at home. Most Dachshunds are chowhounds and can be motivated by food, especially soft treats. Just remember that the piece you offer doesn't have to be very large. You want a trained dog, not an overweight one.

Coming When Called

While you won't be doing formal recalls, the puppy should know his name and should come when called. Offer treats and call your puppy. Sound happy and excited. If his attention wanders, run away from your puppy, calling his name. When he comes, give him a treat and praise him. Never call your puppy for punishment or for something he may find unpleasant. Call him to dinner, not to show him an accident on the rug. If it's time to do his nails, go and get

Of course you're going to keep your belongings out of reach of curious puppies and of course you'll just use dog toys and not old socks or shoes as toys. However, if your Dachshund should get a sock or a nylon stocking or a slipper, the leave it command will prevent a crazy game of tag and may also save your slipper.

him and pick him up. No matter how frustrated the puppy may make you when you're in a hurry and he won't come in, when you do get him, be gentle and praise him. He must always associate good things with obeying the come command.

Teaching Sit

Sitting is probably the easiest thing you can teach a puppy. Hold a treat in front of the dog and slowly move it back over the top of his head. Don't hold it too high or he'll be tempted to jump up. As the treat moves back, give the sit command. The puppy will sit as he tries to follow the treat with his eyes and nose. The instant he sits, give him the treat and tell him how wonderful he is. Keep practicing until he will sit without the treat.

Teaching Stay

Next, you might want to teach your Dachshund to stay. Start with your Dachshund sitting on your left. Place your open palm in front of his nose and give the stay command. Move one step directly in front of your Dachshund, then move back beside him and praise. Gradually extend the amount of time you are in front of him before you release him. As he seems to understand the command, move backward a step or two. If he breaks from the sit, gently

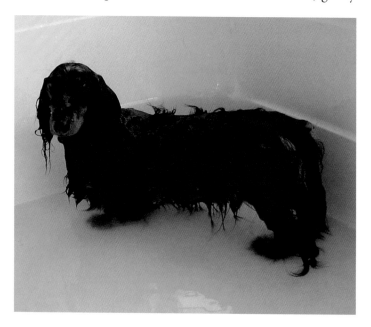

Stand can be a useful request when you're bathing your Dachshund.

replace him, repeat the stay command, and step away. Don't try to go too fast, don't lose your temper, and keep the lesson short and happy. Always end on a positive note.

Teaching Down

Down is a little harder. Many books and many instructors will tell you that once your dog is sitting, you just take a treat and slowly move it down toward his feet and out a bit. The dog will slide into the down. I've seen this work with many breeds, but I've also noticed that many small breeds just pop right up onto all four feet. I don't know if it's the short legs or what.

One of the best ways to teach down to a Dachshund is to teach him a few other commands first, so he understands the concept of learning something. If you have decided to use a clicker, this is one of the benefits. Dogs trained with a clicker seem to realize that there is something you want them to do. They will frequently try everything they know to get you to click and treat. Teach him a sit. Teach a stay. Teach him to walk nicely, even if you won't ever require a perfect heel position. Then, try a down.

First, tell your Dachshund to sit. Hold a treat in your hand, and move it slowly down and away as you give the command to down. If he slides into the down, terrific. Give him lots of praise and the treat. Instead of sliding into the down, he may jump up and go after the hand holding the treat. Don't let him get the treat. He may paw at your hand, or even nibble at it, trying to get the treat. He may sit again. Be patient. Eventually, he will lie down, and that's when you quickly give him the treat and praise him.

Teaching Stand

Stand can also be a useful command. You can use it when you're grooming your Dachshund, or when he's at the veterinarian or when he comes in with muddy feet and you want to wipe them off. If you think you might want to someday show your Dachshund in conformation, you'll need this skill then. Standing for examination is also one of the obedience exercises.

When your Dachshund is seated, take a treat, show it to him, and move it forward from his nose a bit, saying, "Stand" at the same time. When he moves into the stand, praise him, or click, and give him the treat.

Train as You Play

Another way to teach your Dachshund is to name the actions as you play with your Dachshund. If your Dachshund will fetch, throw a ball and tell him to "fetch" or "take it." When he brings it back, tell him to "leave it" or "drop it." Work on having him put it in your hand. You can do this with anything your dog may have—a toy, a bone, a sock. I teach my dogs to "leave it" with almost everything. If there's three feet of snow in the backyard and a Dachshund has a toy in his mouth, you'll want him to leave that toy in the house before he goes out. You won't want to have to dig through the snow to find it, or let it stay hidden until spring. Also, if your dog happens to find a dead critter and decides he'd like to bring it indoors, you won't want to have to pry it from his jaws. You'll want him to leave it.

Keep Training Fun for Both of You

No matter what method or combination of methods you use to train your Dachshund, remember to keep sessions short and positive. Three or four 5-minute sessions are better than one long session. Patience is also important. Don't lose your temper with your puppy, and a sense of humor also helps. Remember that even games can be a way to teach your dog. (Try putting your dog on a stay, going to another room, and calling him.) Don't expect too much at first, but eventually your Dachshund will be doing a sit-stay while you're out of sight.

TRAINING WITH A CLICKER

Clicker training has become very popular and is a good way to train your puppy using only positive methods. The training clickers are available at most pet supply stores.

The clicker marks the behavior at the instant it occurs. There's no delay, as there might be with a word of praise and a treat. Also, the clicker sound is the same every time. There's no edge of impatience, no variation in volume or tone. You can achieve the same results with a word instead of a click, but it has to be a word you use only when training, and you have to say it immediately when the dog gives you the desired response, and you have to try to say it exactly the same way every time. A clicker is much easier.

In the Beginning

To start, get your puppy used to the idea that when he hears the click, he will get a treat. Click and treat several times so the puppy makes the connection between clicker and treat. This is called "charging the clicker," and it won't take long for your Dachshund to figure out the connection between a click and a treat.

You may want to start by luring your dog, that is, using the food to lead, or lure, your dog into doing what you want—for instance, luring the dog into a sit by holding a treat slightly above and over his head. When he sits, click and give him the treat. It may take a little practice to get your timing right. Also, with clicker training, there is no coercion at all. No pressure on the neck or shoulders or rump, no positioning of the legs or body.

While this is a legitimate way to use the clicker, you don't want to always lure. If you only lure, your Dachshund won't offer behaviors on his own, which is what you want. You want your dog to be thinking about learning, which seems to be what happens with clicker training. You can almost see the light bulb go on over your dog's head when he realizes that you want him to do something. He'll actively try to figure out just what that something is so that you'll click and treat.

The important thing with a clicker is the timing. Whenever your puppy does something you want him to do, click and treat.

Shaping Behavior

Shaping a behavior starts by watching your dog, and clicking when he begins to or does something you want him to do. For instance, you want to teach your Dachshund to lie

If you want to pursue more formal training with your Dachshund, you should search out a trainer you want to work with.

down on a specific rug or mat. If it helps, you can put your Dachshund on a lead to keep him in the area, but no hauling or guiding. Just stand there with your dog on a loose lead. If your Dachshund walks over the mat, click and treat. If he happens to sit or lie down, click and give more treats.

The first time or two, you may be rewarding just the walking over the mat, but eventually he will realize that being on the mat earns him treats. Then treat only when he sits, and finally, only when he lies down. If you've taught him to sit and down earlier, chances are he'll be trying these behaviors to see if he gets a reward. Name the action by saying, "Go to your place" or "Go to bed" or whatever you want to say. Remember to be consistent.

The thing to remember about clicker training is that you must click when your dog is doing the behavior you want. If you have an instructor in your area who uses clicker training, talk to her about how to use it best. Read a book or two on the subject. It may take you awhile to learn it yourself, but it will work, and it won't take your Dachshund long to understand it. Besides basic obedience, clicker training can be used in agility training as well as almost any other area of dog training.

Remember that you'll need lots of treats if you're clicker

training. I cut up lots of a soft treat into tiny little bits. Cheese, hot dogs, or baked chicken are all good choices. It's not unusual to go through 30 to 50 tiny treats in a session. Vary the number of treats you give as well. Don't always give just one. If your dog has mastered a new behavior, give him a "jackpot." That is, give him five or six treats, one at a time. Next time, go back to one, then maybe two. This keeps your dog alert and eager.

Don't get frustrated if you can't seem to coordinate your clicking and your treating at first. With practice, you'll improve. It's not unusual to treat and click at first, and it's not a major crime. Your dog will continue to learn, even if you're not perfect. Pretty soon, you will have conditioned yourself to click or praise and treat. The last time I went to a groomer to get my dog's nails cut, I said thank you and dropped a dog treat into her hand!

Capturing is when you click for the final result. You see the dog do something, decide it's something you'd like him to do on command, and you click.

TRAINING BEYOND THE BASICS

With patience, your dog's favorite treat, and a good book or two, you should be able to teach household manners to your dog. If more formal training appeals to you, you can start it on your own, but eventually, if you are thinking of any of the performance sports, you will want to find a professional trainer to help you. Class situations are a good way to both socialize your dog and get him used to distractions. If you've gotten to the point where you want a formal class setting, or you want a trainer to come to you for private lessons, do some homework of your own before you sign up for lessons.

Finding a Class

First, decide what kind of a class you want. Do you just want to teach your dog to sit, stay, come, and walk on a slack lead? Are you hoping to use your dog for therapy work? Are you after more structured lessons that will prepare you for competition-level obedience? Does agility appeal to you? In obedience, your dog works close to you most of the time. In agility, your dog works away from you. Think about what you want from a class before you waste time and money on lessons that don't meet your needs.

Many local kennel clubs sponsor training lessons. In my hometown, the animal shelter offers regular 8-week sessions. Pet superstores or boarding kennels may offer classes, as well. Before you enroll, get some information on the instructor. How long have they been teaching? What breed of dog do they have? What methods do they use in training? Clicker training is gaining in popularity, and if you find a good instructor, it's a wonderful way to train your dog, but there are other methods that work as well.

If possible, see if you can attend a class as an observer. What is the instructor like with the dogs? Stay away from anyone who advocates hitting the dog, or lifting him off his feet by the lead. Your Dachshund doesn't need that, and neither do you.

How large is the class? The larger the class, the less individual attention you'll receive. Classes of more than 10 or 12 dogs might work if the dogs are already trained to some degree and are working on advanced training, but for beginners, the smaller the class, the better. This is true for agility training as well. The larger the class, the less time you and your Dachshund will have to practice.

Talk to friends and neighbors who may have taken obedience classes. See if your veterinarian knows of a class. If you want private lessons, get referrals. Talk to people who've hired a particular instructor.

Once you've signed up for a class, try to attend every session, and do your homework. One training session a week will not teach your Dachshund what you want him to know. You have to devote the time to daily training sessions. But remember, in spite of your care in selecting your trainer, if things aren't working—if the trainer is too rough, or doesn't control the class and you feel your dog might be in danger, or for any reason you are uncomfortable or unhappy—leave. You may not get a refund, but your dog's well-being should be your first concern.

PROBLEM BEHAVIORS
Digging
There may be times when your Dachshund does something you'd rather he didn't do. Many times a sharp "no!" or redirecting the dog to something that is permitted will take care of the problem. Almost all puppies will dig a bit, but it's something they usually outgrow. Dachshunds, of course, are supposed to dig, and they may dig their entire

lives. If your dog enjoys digging, designate a special area of the yard for digging. You might even want to create his own little sandbox. If he digs outside of his special spot, distract him with a toy and lead him to the correct spot. Lightly bury a few smelly treats in the permitted spot and when he digs them up, praise him. Sometimes dogs dig because they are bored. Play with your dog in the yard, or supply a toy or a bone that he enjoys.

Jumping Up

Jumping can be a bad habit, and one that is easily learned. People with small dogs usually don't mind if their dog jumps on them. Dachshunds are small and generally won't knock you down. It's easier to pet a small dog when he jumps up. But, you might not be as happy about the jumping if you're wearing good clothes and your Dachshund has muddy feet. Besides, let's face it, not all your friends will think your dog is as cute as you do. Teach your

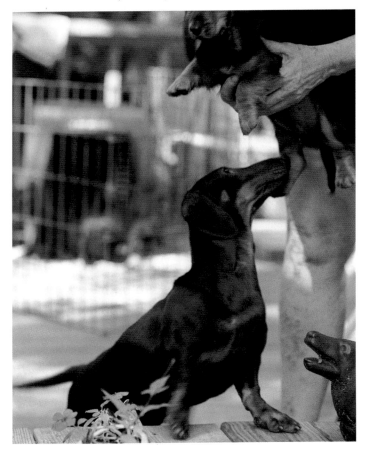

Training your dog to sit when greeting other people or even other dogs is extremely beneficial.

dog to jump up on you on command, if you want to. Otherwise, discourage him. If you have a friend or relative who is a frequent visitor, get them to help.

If your Dachshund jumps up, have your friend turn sideways and ignore the dog. Tell your dog to sit. When he does, have your friend pet him. Only give him attention when he sits, not when he is jumping. Dachshunds love attention. If you pay attention to him when he jumps up, you are reinforcing that behavior.

Barking

Dachshunds have a good, sharp warning bark, and any dog may bark out of boredom if he is left alone too long. Your Dachshund shouldn't be left outdoors unattended for long periods of time, but if he barks every time he is in the yard, even if for only a few minutes, it can become annoying. Consider installing a solid fence. Dogs rarely bark at things they can't see. If that's not possible, consider planting shrubs to screen the sidewalk or neighbor's yard. Give your dog interesting toys, or play with him yourself when he's in the yard.

Many people use invisible fencing and like it very much, but for a small dog, I prefer tangible fencing of some kind. Invisible fencing may very well keep your Dachshund in your yard, but it won't keep out a stray that might wander by. Dachshunds are just like any other dog; they will probably bark at passing dogs, and they will defend their territory. Unfortunately, their size means they will more than likely lose a battle with a larger dog. Fence your yard with fencing tall enough to keep out bigger dogs who might be a threat to your dog.

Indoors, if your Dachshund is barking more than you'd like, there are a couple of ways you can curb the barking. One way is to teach your dog to bark on command. Once he knows how to bark on command, you can also teach a command to stop the barking. When your dog barks, click

Anxiety Barking

If the problem is that your dog barks when no one is home, it may be because he is anxious. This can take a long time to correct. Start by leaving the house. Close the door, then re-enter immediately. Praise the dog and treat. Leave again. Count to five. Go back in. This is a slow process, but eventually, your dog will realize that you are not leaving for good.

and treat. Name the action. Then choose a word that tells him to be quiet. When he does stop, click and treat. If your dog barks every time someone comes to the door, get a friend to help you by coming to the door. You may appreciate the fact that your dog lets you know someone is at the door, but then he should stop when you tell him to. Have your friend knock on the door. When your Dachshund stops barking at your command, open the door. Have your friend treat your dog. Repeat the process.

Challenging Pack Position

As was mentioned, dogs are pack animals. Sometimes dogs try to take over as pack leader. They may refuse to move when you want them to. They may growl or snarl if they are in a chair or on a bed and you want to move them. They may become very possessive of food or toys. You'll need to take back the leadership. This means nothing for free. Your dog must earn everything. He must sit and stay before he eats. He must wait until you go through a door—and no more sleeping on the bed.

If your dog is genuinely aggressive or possessive over food or what he sees as his territory, if he snaps or growls at family members, see your veterinarian first. Your pet may

One method of discouraging unwanted behavior is to completely ignore it. If your dog jumps up to greet you, turn away from him, fold your arms across your chest, and do not make eye contact. Only respond to the behavior you want, such as sitting or moving away. Respond calmly, so as not to excite your dog into other unwanted behaviors.

Be careful not to let the pack—or a pack mentality—take over.

Watching how dogs interact and play with each other can teach you how to communicate better with them.

not appear to be in pain but if there's a physical problem, he may be snapping or growling to warn you away from touching a particular area of his body that hurts. If there's nothing wrong with your Dachshund physically, you may want to contact an animal behavior specialist, which is not the same as a dog trainer. There are many good trainers who are not behavior specialists. Depending on the severity of the problem, a good trainer may be able to help you, even if she isn't a behavior specialist.

If you find you really need a behavior specialist, start your search by talking to your veterinarian and people at your local kennel club. Unfortunately, there is no national standard for certification at this point, so you'll need to consider credentials and get references. Ask to talk to former clients of the specialist. Other helpful organizations are the American Veterinary Society of Animal Behavior or the International Association of Animal Behavior Consultants.

LEARNING EVERYDAY WORDS

Dogs can learn the meaning of many of the words we use everyday. They easily learn the commands we teach, like "sit," "stay," "down," "come," "wait," "off," "take it," and "leave it." If we make the effort, they'll learn to respond to words like "shake," "roll over," "high five," "beg," and any number of other words. People who run their Dachshunds in agility have taught their dogs the names of the obstacles, such as "tunnel" and "chute."

Without our even making any effort at all our dogs quickly learn words like "dinner," and "cookie," and "walk." They know the words "bed time," and many, many more. My parents had a very sensitive dog who, as a puppy, enjoyed digging holes in the backyard. My parents scolded him, telling him, "no digging." He was so affected by the words that for the rest of his life, my parents had to spell the words "dig" and "digging" or he would think he was being scolded.

Service dogs learn many commands specific to the needs of their owners. We can all agree that our dogs know at least some verbal language. And we know some of theirs. If our dog whines, we may know he wants to go out, or that he is afraid of thunder. If he barks and stares at the cupboard door, he wants a dog biscuit. When a dog drops a toy at your feet and looks expectantly at you, you know he wants you to throw the toy. But what about other types of communication? What about body language? Dogs are masters at interpreting body language. They "read" other dogs as well as humans. Let's start with a dog's body language; what they can tell from looking at another dog, and what you can learn by watching theirs.

Not all dogs have tails, and some tails just don't function quite like others. There are certain tail positions that can tell you about what a dog is feeling or thinking. Let's start with a tail tucked between the legs. A dog with his tail tucked between his legs may be frightened. He is definitely being submissive. He may also be unhappy or unsure of himself. He is telling other dogs—and you, if you are paying attention—that he is no threat to anyone. He will also avert his eyes, plaster his ears back, and hold his head low.

A dog may also be anxious or stressed in this position, and he may be panting.

Dogs who are worried may also sit with one paw raised. A yawn briefly lowers a dog's blood pressure and helps him stay calm. A friend's dog licks his nose repeatedly if he meets another dog on a walk. If she continues to approach the strange dog, or the strange dog gets too close, her dog will snarl and snap. She now recognizes his nose-licking signal, and prevents meeting other dogs.

If a dog is aggressive, everything about him leans forward and gets bigger. Ears will be up and forward, the dog will be

Sometimes, dogs seem to pick up more with body language than with verbal cues. If you lean forward when you are teaching the sit, your dog may sit whenever you stand in front of him and lean forward, without the spoken word "sit."

If your dog is licking his nose, yawning, or shaking himself, he is using signals to break the tension. Look around to see what might have him worried.

on his toes. His hackles will rise. His tail will be up and will be stiff. If the dog is snarling, his nose will be wrinkled. He will be staring. If you meet a dog like this on a walk, don't let your Dachshund say hello. This dog does not want to play. If your dog exhibits these traits, don't let him approach another dog.

Your dog may nudge your hand or lean against you in an effort to get you to pet him, or he may put his paw on your knee. A quick lick on your face means he loves you and recognizes you as the leader. Some dogs will limp as a way to get your attention, especially if they've ever suffered a leg or paw injury and had you fuss over them.

Body Language

Dogs use a play bow to indicate that they are in the mood for a game. They'll use this with both people and other dogs. In a play bow, the front half of the body is lowered so that the forelegs are on the ground, leaving the rear end in the air. The tail will be wagging and the dog may give a high-pitched bark or two. They may pant. If your dog drops a toy at your feet and gives you a play bow, it's time to take a break and enjoy your dog.

The play bow can work both ways. You can play bow to your dog when you want to have a game. Put your hands on your knees, smile, pant, and widen your eyes. I've gotten my dog to respond when she's on the bed by putting my arms flat on the bed and lowering my head. Just remember that if your dog responds to that, it will be with a quick pounce, so be ready to dodge.

Some forms of communication are only between dogs. When male dogs mark bushes and trees and poles with urine they are leaving a message to other dogs about their size, sex, and attitude. Females mark to a lesser extent, but they are also leaving a message. Sniffing their way along a walk is the doggy equivalent of reading a newspaper.

Dogs also love to roll in anything that smells different. If you're lucky, your dog will roll in a patch of mint. If you're not so lucky it will be a dead fish—or worse. Some say that rolling in something pungent is a form of camouflage; dogs are using the scent of another creature to disguise themselves. That may be true, but sometimes I think they just like smells. My male routinely rolls on my husband's shoes.

Dachshunds communicate with each other and with us using all their senses.

As much as dogs depend on body language to communicate with other dogs, they are also close observers of human body language. Standing tall and looming over a dog is a sign of dominance when another dog does it, and also when you do it. When you stand tall, or lean over your dog, or even put your arm across his back, you are saying you are dominant; that you are the boss. Conversely, if a strange dog is nervous and shy, you can help the introductions along by crouching down, turning sideways to appear smaller, and not making eye contact. Staring is a form of both dominance and aggression.

Obedience competitors have to be very careful not to move in a certain way, as it may be a cue to the dog. Even the slight drop of a shoulder can be a cue to a dog. That's why hand signals are often incorporated into training. The dog quickly learns both cues. I've noticed that my own dog, when heeling, will sometimes wait to sit until I turn my head slightly. It was an unconscious gesture on my part, but she quickly learned that it means sit.

ADVANCED TRAINING AND ACTIVITIES

F O R   Y O U R   D A C H S H U N D

You may never want to do more with your Dachshund than have him accompany you on your walks around the neighborhood or travels around the world. But it's nice to know that there are many other activities in which you and your Dachshund can participate and even compete.

The Dachshund was bred to be a tenacious hunting dog, going after such fierce vermin as badgers and groundhogs in their lairs. These instincts live on in your dog, and he has a strong prey drive along with a "bring it on" attitude when it comes to a challenge. This may make some advanced training you take on more difficult than if you were working with a retriever or spaniel (dogs bred to be more in service to their owners), but it makes the accomplishments particularly rewarding.

The activities in which you and your Dachshund can compete range from a basic good manners test to highly competitive field trials. This chapter will introduce you to those activities. If they interest you, check the resources in the back of this book for the contact information and get involved. You and your Dachshund will really enjoy it.

CANINE GOOD CITIZEN

You might want to think about getting a CGC title on your dog. CGC stands for Canine Good Citizen, and it is a title awarded by the American Kennel Club to any dog who passes a test for good manners and basic obedience given by a certified evaluator. There are ten different steps to the test. Your dog must allow a stranger to approach, and he must sit quietly and allow the person to pet him. He must allow someone to groom him—you supply the brush or comb and someone runs it lightly over your Dachshund's body. You'll be required to walk your dog on a loose lead through a crowd of people. You will also be asked to have your dog perform a sit, then a down, and then you leave your dog; the dog must stay until you call him. Your dog will also be tested on how he reacts to distractions.

Since many people who have their dog tested for the CGC are also interested in therapy dog work, the distractions are frequently wheelchairs, or a person on crutches or using a walker. The crutches may be thrown to the ground, or the walker may be knocked over to see how well your dog recovers from being startled. Finally, you must tie your dog or hand him to someone

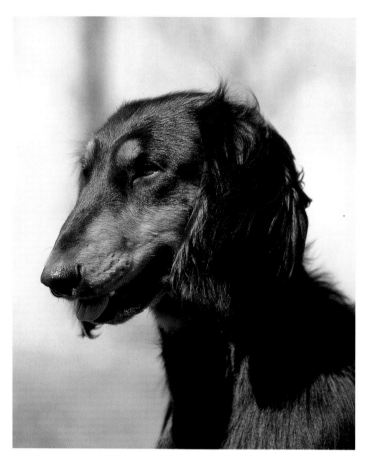

One of the things a Dachshund who's competing in obedience must have mastered is the sit-stay command.

to hold and go out of sight for three minutes. Your dog may move, but he must not whine, bark, or pull to go after you. If you have taken any obedience lessons at all, your dog should be able to pass the CGC test.

FORMAL OBEDIENCE

If your dog passes the CGC test or you have been enjoying obedience classes, you may want to consider earning obedience titles. Most Dachshunds are so food motivated that basic obedience training is fairly quick, but they also get bored easily. Keep training sessions short and positive. If you have not been taking formal classes, you may want to consider them if you are going to compete in formal obedience trials. An instructor will know the best way to teach specific exercises, and attending classes will get your dog used to other dogs. Also, when practicing the long sits and downs, it is better to do so in a group as it simulates actual trial conditions.

Working With Distractions

The group exercises are one of the reasons a class situation is helpful. Besides getting your dog used to other dogs, your instructor may introduce distractions to proof your dog. The instructor may bounce a ball or knock over a chair or walk another dog across the floor. If your dog can handle classroom distractions without breaking his sit or stay, the odds are he will remain in position in the ring.

The Companion Dog Level

The first obedience degree is the Companion Dog title (CD). To be awarded a CD, your dog must qualify under three different judges. A qualifying score is 170 out of a possible 200 points. Also, your dog must win at least half of the points awarded for each exercise. The exercises your dog must pass are: heel on lead and figure eight (40 points), stand for examination (30 points), heel off lead (40 points), the recall (30 points), long sit (30 points), and the long down (30 points).

For heeling on lead, the judge will call out instructions, such as right turn, fast, slow, normal, and halt, and you and your dog must follow these commands, with your dog remaining always in a heel position. The figure eight consists of walking with your dog in a figure-eight pattern around two stewards. On the stand for examination, you remove your lead, command your dog to stand and stay, and move six feet away while the judge lightly touches your dog. Then, you return to the dog's side.

Heel free is just what it sounds like; you again follow the judge's directions, only this time your Dachshund is off lead. For the recall, you will place your Dachshund on a sit-stay, and walk about 35 feet from your dog, then turn to face him. At the judge's signal, you will call your dog, who should move rapidly to sit in front of you. At another signal from the judge, you will command your dog to move into the heel position.

The group exercises are the long sit and the long down. The long sit lasts for one minute; the long down for three. In both of these exercises, competitors line up with their dogs. Armbands and leads are placed behind the dogs. At the command from the judge, you place your dog in either the sit or down, and walk to the far side of the ring, turn, and face your dog. Your dog must remain in either the sit or

In 2004, 51 Dachshunds earned Companion Dog titles; 10 earned Companion Dog Excellent titles; and 1 earned a Utility Dog title. Will your dog be next?

down position, depending on which position the exercise calls for, until you have returned to his side and the judge has ended the exercise with the words, "exercise finished."

The Companion Dog Excellent Level

If you and your dog work well as a team and you both enjoy practicing as well as competing, it shouldn't take long to get your CD. Then it's time to try for a Companion Dog Excellent title (CDX). Once again, you must qualify under three different judges; a qualifying score is 170 out of 200, but for a CDX, the exercises change. You will still be asked to follow a heeling pattern and do a figure eight, but this time, it's all off lead for 40 points.

There is another recall, but this time, when you call your dog, at the judge's signal, you must down your dog as he comes toward you. At another signal, you recall your dog, and he continues to sit in front of you. This is the drop on recall and is worth 30 points.

The long sits and downs are longer, with the sit being for three minutes, and the down being for five, and after you have positioned your dog and walked away, you are led out of the ring and out of sight for the required time. The long sit and the long down are each worth 30 points.

To earn a CDX your dog must also retrieve and jump. Dog supply stores and catalogs will have just the right size dumbbell for your Dachshund. During the trial, your dog must retrieve on the flat, for 20 points, and retrieve over a high jump for 30 points. The jump height is based on the height of your dog at the withers. Dachshunds usually jump 12 inches.

The other required jump is the broad jump, which is twice as long as the height of the high jump. If your Dachshund jumps a high jump of 12 inches, he will need to jump a broad jump that is 24 inches long. The broad jump is worth 20 points. Again, class work may be just the thing.

Teaching your dog to jump consistently should be taught slowly. Dachshunds may easily jump higher to get on the couch or into your lap, but formal training should start with a very low jump, getting your dog used to jumping on command. Pushing your dog can lead to injury and may make him refuse to jump at all.

The Utility Dog Level

Competition for Utility Dog (UD) changes drastically. Classes no longer include long sits and downs. There is a heeling pattern to follow, but this time there are no verbal commands. All commands must be hand signals. Included in this exercise is the command to stand your dog, leave your dog, and at the judge's signals, to drop (or down) your dog, sit, come, and finish (return to heel position), all with hand signals. This is the signal exercise and is worth 40 points.

Next comes scent discrimination. In scent discrimination, your dog is asked to select the article with your scent on it. Scent articles come in sets of two, with one set being entirely metal, and one set being leather. Each article is numbered. Although technically, they may be of any shape, the articles are usually small dumbbells in the appropriate material, which makes it easier for the dog to pick up.

During a trial the judge will indicate which number article in each set will be used. These two articles are set aside. The remaining eight articles are placed on the ground about 20 feet from you and your dog. With your back to the articles, you will then place your scent on either the metal or leather article, using your hands. Without touching the article, the judge will then take it, either on his clipboard, or with tongs, and place it with the other articles on the ground. At the signal, you and your dog will turn to face the articles, and you will send your dog to retrieve the article you have handled. The process is repeated with the next article.

The next exercise is the directed retrieve. In this exercise, while you and your dog have your back to the steward, he or she drops three white gloves in a line. The judge then has you turn to face the gloves and once you are turned, indicates which glove your dog is to retrieve.

The next exercise is the moving stand and examination. In this exercise, the dog heels beside you until the judge gives you the command to stand your dog. At this point, without stopping, you command your dog to stand while you continue another 10 to 12 feet and then turn and face your dog. The judge examines your dog, and then you call the dog to heel.

The directed jump has two jumps, the high jump, such as is used in CDX competition, and the bar jump, which is a

Sets of three Dachshund-sized gloves may be purchased from catalogs or booths at dog shows, so you don't need to worry about your Dachshund tripping on a huge work glove or about buying two pairs of gloves and throwing one glove away.

single bar supported by two uprights. In this exercise, you send the dog away from you to the far side of the ring. At the command sit, your dog will turn to face you and sit. When the judge indicates either high or bar jump, you give a signal, and your dog must jump the designated jump. This is then repeated for the second jump.

Utility Dog Excellent is the next title up the obedience ladder, and may be earned by achieving a qualifying score in both Open B and Utility B classes at ten separate approved events.

The Obedience Trial Champion

Ready for more obedience? Then you're ready to try for an obedience trial championship, or OTCH. To put an OTCH on your dog, you must win 100 points from either the Open B or Utility B class. Points are based on the number of dogs you beat. You can only win points if you are in first or second place in your class. In addition, you must, under three different judges, win a first place in Open B over six dogs or more, and a first in Utility B over three dogs or more, and another first in either class, under the listed conditions.

If obedience sounds just right for you and your Dachshund, get the booklet of official regulations from the AKC, find an instructor you like, and enjoy!

At a dog show, your Dachshund will be evaluated against the judge's idea of an ideal Dachshund according to the breed's standard.

THE CONFORMATION RING (DOG SHOWS)

Conformation judging is what most people think of when they think of a dog show. The Group and Best in Show judging is what you see on television when a show such as the Westminster Kennel Club dog show is televised. Dog shows are held year round, indoors and out, and may range in size from entries of under 100 to over 3,000.

In the early years of dog shows, all the shows were benched, that is, all dogs of the same breed were together in the benching area, and were there all day. The dogs sat on the benches with their owners so people could see them. Today, there are only six benched shows left in the country. All other shows are unbenched, which means you can arrive anytime before your dog is to be judged and may leave as soon as the judging is finished.

For people who need to drive back and forth, this type of show can save on hotel bills and meals, but it isn't as easy to find someone to talk to if you want to research a breed of dog. At benched shows, the dog must remain on his bench for the hours of the show, unless the dog is being groomed, exercised, fed, or shown.

The Westminster Kennel Club show is benched. It is one of the most prestigious shows in the country and entries usually close within minutes of them opening. Because of the space restrictions, only 2,500 dogs may enter this show, and it is now open only to champions.

Is Your Dog Show Quality?

You might not have thought much about showing your Dachshund when you got him, but chances are your breeder discussed with you whether or not your puppy was potentially show quality. Show quality means your dog has no disqualifying faults as discussed in the standard, and that he is structurally sound and built as a Dachshund should be. Another quality to look for in a show dog is personality. Most Dachshunds have plenty of personality, but some may be a bit more laid back than others. A competitive show dog loves the crowd and has attitude. You will sometimes hear a judge say that a particular dog was "asking for the win." That is a dog who is confident and happy in the ring. If you think you might enjoy showing, ask your breeder or someone who

Find a Mentor
As with other dog-related activities, it is possible to learn from books and from trial and error, but it is much, much easier if you can find someone to help you. A dog show mentor can save you time and money and may mean the difference between giving up and persevering.

The Dachshund is a table breed, meaning that at a dog show the judge examines him on a grooming table. The judge also watches the dog move and stand on the ground.

knows Dachshunds to reevaluate him. If their opinion is positive, give it a try!

Many kennel clubs offer handling classes, and this an excellent place to learn about how to gait and stack your dog and what kind of collar and lead to use, as well as bait. With my first show dog I had both a mentor in the breed of the dog, and I also attended classes in handling. The formal class gave my dog socialization with other dogs and I received pointers on how to place my dog on the table, move at the proper pace, and learn the different patterns of movement that the judge might request. (In order to see your dog in action, the judge may ask for a down and back, a triangle, or an L. You'll want to practice this before you actually show your dog.)

Whether or not you attend formal classes, you may want to attend a match or two before you actually enter a show. A match is an event put on by a dog club. It is run like a dog show, but the dogs can't win any points. It is frequently more casual than a show, and a judge at a match is more likely to give you advice than a judge at a licensed show would. Match entry fees are also much less than those of a show, usually being around five dollars.

Preparing for the Show Ring

When I first started showing, my mentor gave me breed specific tips in terms of what kind of collar and lead work best, a good speed to move at for gaiting, and ideas for bait, the food used to get a dog's attention in the ring. My mentor showed me how to groom for the ring, and also helped me with entry forms and suggested judges who might like my dog. This last tip can definitely help you save time and money. An experienced dog show competitor keeps a file on judges and what they may or may not like in a particular dog. If your dog's movement is not the best, there's no point in showing to a judge who considers movement very important. If your dog's head fits the standard in every way, there is probably a judge who is looking for just that feature.

Another advantage to having a mentor is that you and she can travel together to your first few shows. It's a lot less intimidating when you are traveling with someone who knows where to go and what to do.

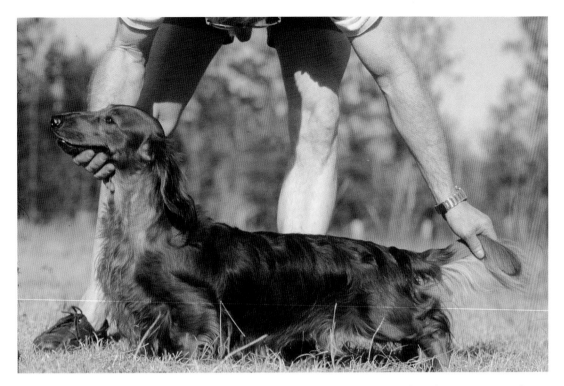

At a Show

So, let's pretend to do just that...go to a show. You've purchased the proper show lead, as recommended by your mentor, and you've attended classes, so you understand how to move your dog at the correct pace around the ring and how to stack your dog on the table, so the judge can examine him. You've cooked hot dogs or liver or chicken, or whatever treats your dog loves, so that you can get his attention in the ring. Your dog is also in good show condition, that is, well groomed and physically ready. A Dachshund isn't a working dog, but he still should not be soft and flabby, he should get enough regular daily exercise to give him good muscle tone.

Handling classes, mentors, and fellow dog show friends can all help you learn to handle and evaluate your Dachshund for the show ring.

Packing for the Show

It's time to pack the car for the show. The most important item, of course, is your dog. But how is he to travel? You'll need his crate in the car, and you may want an extra one for your hotel room and maybe even one at the show site. Pack your tack box, which holds all your grooming supplies: Brushes, treats, show leads, spray bottles of water, baby wipes, waterless shampoo, and whatever else you need to make sure your dog looks his best for the judge.

You'll need your grooming table, a grooming smock and don't forget extra towels. You'll want one for on the grooming table, one for wiping off mud, drying feet, (maybe drying the entire dog if it rains), or a couple for extra bedding in case what is in the crate gets dirty; you can never have too many towels.

A wire exercise pen is a good idea, too, so your Dachshund has a place other than his crate to move around in, and if the grounds are muddy or very crowded, he has a place for elimination without the need for a walk. Water is essential. Carry your own water from home to prevent any digestive upset. If the show is in the summer, make sure you have whatever you need to keep your Dachshund cool. There are wonderful crate pads that keep pets cool, as well as special little coats you can wet down to keep your Dachshund from overheating. Some people use ice packs wrapped in a towel.

You'll also want to take food, of course, if you are going for more than the day. You may want to carry some for yourself as well as the dog. Dog show food is usually of the hot dog and hamburger variety, if it exists at all. A small cooler packed with some sandwiches or snacks can make your day more pleasant.

Don't even think about entering your dog in a show if he is not groomed to perfection, as this miniature Wirehaired is.

What Will You Wear?

Consider your wardrobe as you pack. You want to look neat and well groomed, but you should also be prepared for whatever weather you may encounter. At an indoor show, this isn't such a concern, but at an outdoor show, you may encounter heat, cold, rain, mud, and/or wind. Follow the Scout motto and be prepared.

Don't forget your paperwork. Always carry your dog's current rabies certificate. I've made a copy and keep it in my tack box. You'll also want your judging schedule, so you'll know where you're supposed to be and at what time, and your dog's entry form, which is usually your ticket to enter the show. Remember to take any directions you need to get to the show site, and allow yourself plenty of time to get there. You've paid from 20 to 25 dollars to enter your dog in the show; make sure you don't miss your ring time.

When You Get to the Show

You've made your list, checked it twice, and the car is loaded and ready to go. If you are going to an indoor show, there will usually be an unloading area near a building door. You can unload your grooming table and supplies, and then move your car to the parking area. It is a good idea to get to

What to Wear When Showing

You must look neat and well groomed when you show, but you should also be prepared for the weather. This can include heat, cold, rain, mud, and/or wind. Be prepared: Throw your raincoat in the car, no matter what the long-range weather forecast says. Carry extra shoes and a hat. Flat, comfortable shows are a must for both men and women; you don't want to risk falling in the ring, and you're going to be on your feet for most of the day, so you don't want tired feet. Men should wear a blazer and tie; women should wear a dress or skirt, although a pants suit is acceptable. Skirts should be loose enough to move freely in, without being too full. A billowing skirt can obscure the judges' view of your dog, and may even interrupt your dog's gait if the skirt blows across his face. Solid colors that make a good contrasting background to your dog are a good choice. With Dachshunds, greens, light-to-medium blues and reds are good choices, and with red or cream Dachshunds, the darker colors make a good background. If you have a black Dachshund, avoid black or navy blue.

If you're showing in a performance event, you'll still want those comfortable shoes, but women generally wear slacks for performance events. In obedience, contrary to the conformation ring, wear slacks that match as closely as possible the color of your Dachshund. A crooked sit may not be as noticeable if that black Dachshund is next to black slacks.

Agility competition is a little more casual in terms of dress. Wear something you can easily move in as you sprint from obstacle to obstacle. I've seen people compete barefoot and wearing shorts. Whatever works for you and your dog is fine.

the show site early because grooming space fills up fast. Luckily, Dachshunds don't take up much room! At an outdoor show, the grooming area will usually be under a separate tent. Again, there will be a loading and unloading area. If the show site offers large, grassy parking areas with shade, you might want to simply set up your table next to your car; you can work out of your car and avoid unloading everything.

If you decide on this method, make sure you have some sort of awning or sunscreen to keep the car cool. Draping space blankets over the windows keeps out a lot of heat. Never, ever leave your dog unattended in a closed car. Dogs do not perspire like humans do. Their lungs act as a cooling agent. If they are breathing in super hot air, there is no chance for the proper heat exchange, and they will quickly overheat.

Once you're settled, indoors or out, double-check your judging time and find your ring so you know exactly where you'll be going. If it's not too early, pick up your armband from the ring steward. Your armband number is on your entry form; just tell the steward your breed and the number. There will be rubber bands available, so you can secure the band to your upper left arm.

The next thing to do is to groom your dog. You should have already clipped your dog's toenails and foot fur at home and given a bath if needed. Show-site grooming for a Dachshund should be a matter of touchup. Brush and comb thoroughly. If the site is muddy or wet, use waterless shampoo to spot clean. Wipe his feet, and check your dog's eyes, nose, and ears.

Next, you may want to crate your dog until just before you go to the ring, or you may want to head for your ring early. Some dogs show better if they go directly from their crate to the ring; others do better if they have a little time to settle down and get used to the crowd before showing. Experience will tell you. Either way, with or without your dog, try to watch the judge as he judges a few dogs so that you'll be ready for whatever pattern he will use when you gait your dog for him. Does he ask for the first dog to be put directly on the table, or will he ask you to go around the ring first? Knowing ahead of time will save time in the ring and you'll be calmer, which will help both you and your dog.

Putting Your Dog in the Right Class

Now, what class did you and your mentor decide was the best for your dog? Class choices are puppy 6 to 9 months, puppy 9 to 12 months, 12 to 18 months, Novice, American bred, Bred-By-Exhibitor, and Open. Entrants in Novice may not have any points, may not have won more than three first place ribbons from the Novice Class, or may not have won a first place in any other class, except puppy. American bred means the entered dog must have been bred in the United States. In the Bred-By-Exhibitor Class, the owner or co-owner must have bred the dog, or be a member of the immediate family. Any dog may be entered in the Open Class. All classes are divided, with males competing against males, and females competing against females.

Earning a Ribbon

Ribbons are awarded for first through fourth place. The winners of each class, those who got the blue ribbon, then compete with other class winners for Winners Dog or Winners Bitch. The dog who wins winners is the dog who earns one or more points towards a championship.

The Winners Dog and Winners Bitch then go on to compete with any champions entered for the title of Best of Breed. Should either of the winners go Best of Breed they may also win more points. For instance, there may be enough dogs entered to give the Winners Dog three points, but only enough bitches entered to give the Winners Bitch two points. If the bitch should beat the male by going Best of Breed, then she would also receive three points. The point schedule which determines how many dogs you must beat for how many points is broken up into regions, and the show catalog will list this for each breed. To win three, four,

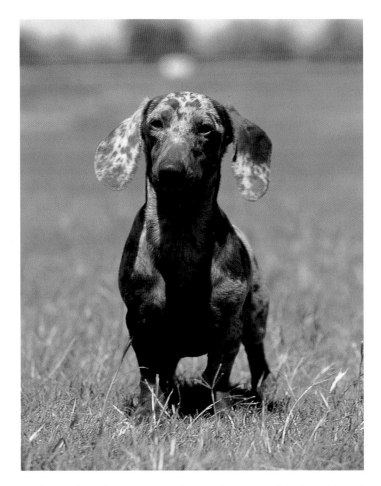

Agility is the fastest-growing sport in dogs because people and dogs love it. This dog perks up at the mere mention of the sport.

or five points is to get a major. A championship is achieved with a total of not less than 15 points, of which the dog must win two majors under two separate judges.

Even if your dog doesn't win, you'll want to watch the entire Dachshund judging, and to cheer on the Best of Breed winner when he competes in the group ring. There are seven groups and the Best of Breed winners from all the entered breeds compete with others of their group. Dachshunds are in the Hound Group. The seven Group winners then compete for the title Best in Show.

Junior Showmanship

Another part of most conformation shows is Junior Showmanship. This is a special class, designed to give younger dog lovers a chance to practice their handling skills. Classes are Novice, for those juniors who have not won three first place awards, with competition present, in a Novice

Class, and Open, for those who have won three first place awards, with competition present, in a Novice Class. Usually, these two classes are further divided into Junior and Senior Classes. Junior classes are for boys and girls who are at least 10 years old and under 14 years old on the day of the show. Senior class is for boys and girls who are at least 14 years old and under 18 years old on the day of the show. The dog being shown must belong to the junior, or to a member of his or her immediate family and must be eligible to be shown in regular conformation or obedience classes. Bitches in season may not be shown.

Dachshunds are one of the breeds in the Hound Group that most actively competes in AKC Agility. Over 180 Dachshunds earned titles in 2004.

AGILITY

If you can barely get your dog to heel, or obedience just doesn't sound like your cup of tea, don't worry; there are lots of other things you can do with your Dachshund! You might want to try agility. Agility is a rapidly growing sport that gives both you and your dog exercise and is fun. Again, it's a good idea to find a class and a good instructor. Agility equipment takes up a lot of room and is fairly expensive to purchase, although if you are at all handy, you can build most of it yourself.

Getting Involved

If you are interested in agility, there are three major organizations in the US—the AKC, the United States Dog Agility Association (USDAA), and the North American Dog Agility Council (NADAC). Each has its own set of rules and regulations. Talk to other people in the sport, and contact the organizations for their rules and regulations, as each organization has slightly different rules, and these rules change periodically.

For instance, NADAC has just eliminated the cleats, or cross bars, on the Teeter-Totter, Dog Walk, and A-Frame, and has lowered the height of the A-frame. And, both NADAC and USDAA have added variations to the standard course. NADAC offers Gamblers where the dog is required to accurately perform obstacles while remaining a required distance away from the handler during part of the class. The Tunnelers class is a numbered course comprised exclusively of tunnels. The Weavers class is a numbered course comprised of tunnels and sets of weave poles. There are both

You've Got to Register to Compete

While conformation showing requires a dog to be registered with the AKC and to be intact, that is, not spayed or neutered, the competition events permit spayed or neutered dogs to compete, and you may also compete with an unregistered dog, as long as you have an ILP number. (ILP stands for Indefinite Listing Privilege.) This number is granted to dog's who are purebred but who were never formally registered for whatever reason. You must submit pictures of your dog to the AKC, and if they agree the dog is the breed you say he is, you will be given an ILP number and be permitted to compete in performance events.

short sets of 6 weave poles and long sets of 10 to 12 weave poles, intermixed with open tunnels on the course. The Touch N Go class is a numbered course comprised of contact obstacles and tunnels. The obstacles can be a mix of tunnels, teeter totters, A-frames, and dog walks.

Both the AKC and NADAC offer classes with lower jump heights for small dogs. If your Dachshund jumps 12 inches but you are worried about injuries or stressing him, you may enter the AKC preferred class, which means 8-inch jumps and an added five seconds to the time to complete the course. NADAC offers lower jump heights to several breeds, including the Dachshund, who is offered an 8-inch jump instead of a 12-inch jump. USDAA offers no lower jump height.

Each organization has three levels of competition. The AKC has Novice, Open and Excellent. USDAA has Starters/Novice, Advanced, and Master. NADAC has Novice, Open and Elite. The AKC also has Jumpers With Weaves (JWW), which is a course with no contact obstacles. It has jumps, weave poles, and may or may not have open and/or closed tunnels. Titles in JWW include Novice, Open, Excellent, and Master Excellent. You can also go on to win agility championships.

About the Obstacles

The main obstacles in an agility course are the A-frame, where the dog goes up one side of the A and down the other; the dog walk, which is a sloping board that leads up to another level board across which the dog walks, and then another sloping board down to the ground; a seesaw; four types of jumps (broad, panel, bar, and tire or window jump); a pause table, where you must, at the judge's direction, either have your dog sit or down for the count of five; an open tunnel; and a closed tunnel, or chute, which consists of an open, rigid entry area, and an expanse of cloth for the exit. The fabric has no support, so the dog must push through it to exit.

The Dachshund's enthusiasm and "can-do" attitude make him an able performer in agility.

Weave poles are the final element and are not a part of an AKC Novice course. The A-frame, the dog walk, and the seesaw are all contact obstacles; that is, they all have a contact zone where the obstacle touches the ground, and it is usually painted yellow. The dog must touch this area as he gets both on and off of the obstacle. This is to ensure that the dog does not leap on or off the obstacle, thus risking injury.

When You're Hooked

Agility is a very challenging and complex sport, but as your dog gains confidence, he will perform with almost the same speed that he chases a ball. This speed can be a problem at advanced levels because the dog may miss the yellow contact zone coming off an obstacle. The best advice is to put in the time at the Novice level, making sure you get a solid contact, so that this does not become a problem at advanced levels. It's also a good idea to wait a bit and not push the dog too hard. A dog may not compete in AKC agility until he is 12 months old, and it is a good idea to wait until he is 18 months to two years old before actually competing. (A dog must be at least 18 months of age to compete in NADAC.) This gives both you and your dog time to get in condition and build up stamina. If you plan to do agility, the weave poles are an obstacle you will definitely want to have in your own backyard. For competitive agility, one class a week is not enough to teach your dog proficiency on the weave poles. A few jumps are also a good idea.

TRACKING

Tracking is another activity you might want to try with your Dachshund. You will need a harness and a tracking lead, which must be between 20 and 40 feet long. You will also need access to some wide-open spaces for laying tracks.

What Is Tracking?

Tracking tests a dog's ability at following a particular scent over various terrains. Variable Surface Tracking (VST) includes pavement as well as to other surfaces, such as gravel and grass. As with obedience titles, there are various levels of tracking. Each level is determined by the number of turns in the trail, the length of the trail, and how long it has aged, before the dog starts the trail. Aging refers to the amount of time between when the trail is laid and the time when the dog is allowed to start tracking. Tracking titles are Tracking Dog (TD), Tracking Dog Excellent (TDX), and Variable Surface Tracking (VST).

When training, take care that the trail is not crossed or otherwise contaminated by scents other than that of the Tracklayer. To begin training, the handler makes a simple trail, crushing the grass and placing a piece of hot dog in each footprint. This marks the trail in three ways; handler scent, crushed vegetation, and hot dog. At the end of the trail, place something the dog will be happy to find. A glove containing more hot dog is a common item, but it could be the dog's favorite toy. Gradually, trails get longer, include turns, and are aged.

The Dachshund Friendship Club

For Dachsie owners who just want to socialize with other Dachshund owners, there's the Dachshund Friendship Club. Membership is less than $20 annually and includes four newsletters. The Friendship Club also holds a spring "fiesta" and a fall "Octoberfest" in Washington Square Park in New York City. For information, e-mail Adrian Milton at doxieking@aol.com.

Earning Titles

To earn the TD title, your dog must follow a track that is at least 440 yards long, has three to five turns, and has been aged at least 30 minutes but no longer than two hours. The track can't cross any paved area or any body of water, and there are two starting flags, one 30 yards from the first, to indicate the direction in which the track was laid. At the end of the track is either a glove or wallet, which the dog must indicate in some way.

For the TDX title, the track increases to at least 800 yards long, has five to seven turns, and has been aged at least three hours but no more than five. For this title, there are four articles to be found along the trail, with only the last one being a glove or wallet, and two cross tracks are laid, trails that cross the main track. There must also be two obstacles in a TDX track. An obstacle may be a stream, a fence, a bridge, a lightly traveled road, or a gully. These obstacles test the dog's ability to continue scenting under different physical and handling conditions, and while overcoming a physical obstacle. The handler is allowed to assist the dog over or under obstacles. With a Dachshund's short legs, this may, indeed, be necessary.

VST tracking tests your Dachshund's ability to track over changing surfaces. A dog must already have a TD or a TDX to compete for a VST. In this test, the trail must cross three different surfaces, with one being vegetation, and the other two a combination of concrete, asphalt, gravel, sand, hardpan, or mulch. The track is aged for three to five hours and must have between four and eight turns. Besides adding to the complexity with different surfaces, tracks should be laid near buildings, which can change the pattern of the scent. Trails may not, however, lead through any building with closed doors and sides.

As with the TDX, there are four articles to be found, but the requirements for these articles are much more exact for the VST. To quote from the AKC booklet on tracking regulations, "Each article shall not be smaller than 2" x 5" nor larger than 5" x 5" and shall weigh no more than eight ounces. There shall be one leather, one plastic (rigid or semi-rigid), one metal, and one fabric article, which shall be handled by the Tracklayer and are to be dropped on the track by the Tracklayer at the points

In 2004, 17 Dachshunds earned AKC tracking titles—16 TDs and 1 TDX. They were the number-two Hound breed to earn them, behind the Basset, with 21 titles.

indicated on the judges' charts. The first article shall be fabric or leather. The last article shall be clearly marked with the number 4."

To complete a tracking title, two judges must certify that the dog has successfully completed the track for any given trail. A Champion Tracker title (CT) is awarded to any dog who has earned all three tracking titles.

FIELD TRIALS

Field trials test your dog's ability to follow a trail, and here is where you'll hear them give voice as they trail the rabbit. In field trials, dogs are run in pairs, or braces, and they are judged on how well they search for and pursue game, accuracy in trailing, obedience to commands, use of voice, and their willingness to follow the rabbit into a burrow. The dogs love this sport, and there's not much training involved.

EARTHDOG TRIALS

Whether competing with one or several Dachshunds, it's your responsibility to make sure they're safe at any event.

Dachshunds can earn three different titles in Earthdog competition, Junior Earthdog (JE), Senior Earthdog (SE), and Master Earthdog (ME). The AKC Earthdog Event tests a dog's willingness to follow prey into their den. A cage containing rats is at the end of the tunnel.

The Introduction to Quarry is an instinct test. You might want to try this first to see if your Dachshund has an interest in going to ground. This test is a 10-foot long tunnel with one 90-degree turn.

For the Junior Earthdog title, a dog must qualify at two different tests under two different judges. There is a 30-foot tunnel and three 90-degree turns. There is an entrance at one end, and a quarry area at the other end, with no additional entrances, exits, or dead ends.

To earn the Senior Earthdog title, the dog must have already earned the JE title and must qualify at three different tests under two different judges. In this test there is a 30-foot main tunnel, three 90-degree turns, a secondary exit and a false den. The secondary exit should be approximately 7 feet in length with one 90-degree turn. The false den will be a side tunnel approximately 4 feet in length with no exit. The false den will have a heavily scented simulated litter/bedding area. The entrance to the den is camouflaged by a 4-inch dirt mound providing a steep 45-degree entrance to the den.

If your Dachshund loves going to ground, now's the time to try for the title Master Earthdog. To earn the ME title, the dog must qualify at four different tests under two different judges. The tunnel setup is the same as for the SE, but with the following modifications: the entrance is not readily visible but is blocked with a removable obstruction. A 20-foot scent line leads to the entrance, but an unscented false den entrance is located midway along the scent line. There is an 18-inch section of the tunnel that constricts to a 6-inch passage. There is an obstacle in the tunnel, which is a 6-inch diameter section of PVC pipe, suspended crossways in the tunnel with 9 inches on each side of the pipe's centerline.

For all these tests there is a time limit, and when the dog reaches the quarry, he is expected to "work" the quarry for a specific amount of time. That is, make every effort to reach the quarry.

SPORTS AND SAFETY

The sport of dogs offers all kinds of competitive events at many different levels. It's great fun to compete with your dog, but keep your best friend's safety in mind, too.

At all dog events, there will be other dogs. Most of these other dogs are used to being out in public and being around other dogs. That doesn't mean that all of the other dogs will be friendly all of the time. Dachshunds are small. A large dog can be intimidating and may be dangerous. Keep your dog on-lead at all times, unless in a ring or exercise pen. If you're moving through a crowd, pick up your Dachshund. I prefer to let my dogs walk on their own four feet whenever possible, but in a crowd, especially one that contains several large dogs, it's better to be safe than sorry. Besides the threat of other dogs, a person could easily step on or trip over your Dachshund.

If you're in obedience and your Dachshund doesn't always hold his stays and you're afraid he might leave the

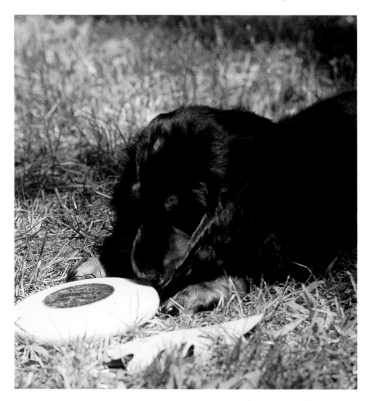

Their short legs won't win them any applause for drama at Frisbee-throwing contests, but it doesn't mean you and your Dachshund can't enjoy a catch, or perhaps a chew.

ring, mention it to the steward before you go in, so they are prepared to block the gate.

Those contact areas on agility equipment are there for a reason, and it's to help prevent injury to your dog. Train your dog to hit the contact areas. I've watched people with very fast dogs bring them to a halt coming off the contact obstacles. Sure, it may cost a second or two in time, but the dog isn't leaping off to a potential injury.

With any event, remember that your Dachshund is very sensitive to heat, and his short nose and face make it harder for him to cool off. If you're showing in conformation, and you keep your Dachshund cool before and after his appearance in the ring, the heat shouldn't be a problem, but with performance events, if the humidity is 90 percent and the temperature is 85 degrees, you may want to pull your entry.

Dachshunds make good therapy dogs because their size is not threatening. A drawback is that they are a bit hard to reach to pet when a person is in a wheelchair or a bed, but you can easily pick up your dog and hold him for the loving attention of those you are visiting.

THERAPY DOGS

If your own tendencies lean more toward couch potato than athlete, maybe therapy work is the niche for you and your Dachshund. Dachshunds are such lovers that therapy work is a wonderful choice for them. Visiting a nursing home doesn't require much physical effort, but the emotional rewards can be tremendous. This is a chance for you to share your wonderful dog with people whose activities have become limited.

There are organizations that register therapy dogs, among them are Therapy Dogs International and the Delta Society. Actually having a registered therapy dog means that your dog has passed a test similar to the Canine Good Citizen test, with the addition of testing your dog around someone in a wheelchair and someone using a walker or crutches or both. The person using the walker or crutches will usually drop them, testing your dog's reaction to strange noises and also to the walker and crutches themselves. If your dog becomes a registered therapy dog, he will have a special ID tag for his collar and may have a laminated wallet card also that you can show. The registering agency will need proof that your dog passed the necessary test, and that all vaccinations are up to date. The agency may provide insurance coverage for visits, and will offer guidelines for taking your dog to hospitals or other health care facilities.

With their loving personalities and convenient size, Dachshunds can make excellent therapy dogs with the proper training.

Your dog doesn't need to be registered to make visits, but it's a good idea to follow many of the guidelines, including checking out to see how your dog will react to wheelchairs and walkers before you make a visit. Take proof of vaccinations with you when you visit, and make sure your dog is well groomed and has had his nails trimmed.

Your dog may or may not be permitted into a person's lap or onto a bed. Check with the facility manager before you allow either of these behaviors. Older people have more delicate skin, and there may be a concern that the dog's nails will bruise or tear the skin. That's why it's so important to make sure your dog's nails are short, and that he is absolutely clean.

ACTIVITIES AT HOME

Dachshunds want to be near you and most will try hard to please you, but if it turns out that you and your Dachshund don't really enjoy any of these activities, don't worry. You can enjoy impromptu games in your own home.

Hide-and-Seek

Almost all dogs enjoy hide-and-seek. Put your Dachshund on a sit-stay (or have a family member hold him). Hide somewhere. In the beginning, maybe just in another room. As your Dachshund gets used to the game, you can hide behind doors or in closets. Call your Dachshund. He'll enjoy trying to find you.

You can also play another kind of hide-and-seek with a treat. At first, use a treat that has a very definite odor, like a small cube of cheese. Keep it in your closed hand, but let your Dachshund smell it. Go to a different room and hide the treat. Again, the first few times you may want to hide it in a simple place, maybe even in the middle of the floor, just to give your dog the idea.

Tricks

You can also teach your dog tricks, like rolling over or giving a high-five. There are several good books out there on how to teach your dog tricks. Clicker training makes it easy to build on those tricks and even create entire routines. Best of all, your Dachshund will love showing off.

Don't really want to do any of this? That's fine. Your Dachshund will be just as happy with regular walks, lots of cuddling, and as many treats as he can beg. The idea is to spend time together and enjoy each other's company.

HEALTH

The health of your Dachshund will be a concern from the day you bring home that cute little puppy until the sad day when you finally say good-bye. It's up to you to provide the best care you can for your dog and to understand some of the issues that will face your dog throughout his life.

Depending on your contract with the breeder, there will be a specified window of time for getting a clean bill of health or returning the puppy to the breeder. The time limit may be anywhere from 48 hours to one month, with the shorter time frame more common.

CHOOSING A VETERINARIAN

First, find a veterinarian that you like and feel comfortable with, one who is willing to discuss your dog's health care with you. If possible, find this veterinarian before you get your puppy.

Ask friends who have pets which veterinarian they go to, and why. If they have a complaint about a particular practice, is it legitimate?

Large Practice or Small?

Think about whether you want to take your dog to a large practice, with multiple doctors, or to a smaller practice. There can be advantages to both. In a small practice, the veterinarian may get to know you and your dog better than if you see different doctors on different visits. The disadvantage is that if your veterinarian is on vacation or ill, a veterinarian from a different practice won't know you at all. In an emergency, that vet won't have any background on your pet. With a larger practice, while a particular veterinarian might not really know you, he will have your pet's entire medical history easily accessible.

Distance may determine which veterinarian you go to. If you've gotten recommendations for more than one practice, you may want the one closest to your home. Or maybe there's a practice where one of the veterinarians has Dachshunds. That may appeal to you. All dogs have health issues particular to their breed and a veterinarian who is familiar with Dachshunds will be more aware of what to look for when he's examining your Dachshund.

How comfortable you are with the veterinarian, support staff, and facilities is more important than proximity to your home.

Consider the practice's response to emergencies. Is there someone on call at night and on holidays? Does the staff seem willing to squeeze you in if there's a sudden problem, or do they brush you off? Are the offices and waiting room clean? Will the veterinarian take the time to explain what he or she is doing?

Be Comfortable With Your Choice

You may not be able to answer all these questions without a visit or two to the office, but if anything makes you uncomfortable, find another veterinarian. Even if everything about the office is perfect, if you aren't happy with the veterinarian for whatever reason, go elsewhere. You want someone who can care for your pet, of course, but you also want someone you are comfortable around, who will talk to you about your pet's care and who will answer your questions. You also want someone who will listen to you. Even the best veterinarian won't know your dog as well as you will. Ideally, you and your veterinarian will be partners, working to keep your dog healthy.

Dachshund puppies are so cute that the veterinary staff will probably pay some extra attention to your puppy before the examination. This will be good for the puppy, as it will give him a pleasant association with the office, not just the memory of a shot.

The First Visit

If your puppy hasn't received all his shots, this initial visit becomes even more important. Both distemper and parvovirus are often fatal in puppies, so this is not a visit to ignore or postpone.

At this first appointment, if you have any concerns at all or any questions about proper health care, ask your vet. If you are uncomfortable about brushing your puppy's teeth, for example, ask for a demonstration and discuss different methods. Ask about flea and tick protection, and about heartworm preventative. Ask if there are any specific health concerns related to your part of the country, such as Lyme disease. Your dog's health will be your responsibility for the next 14 to 16 years, so start off right.

When you bring your puppy home, he should not have any evidence of fleas or ticks and should have been wormed, since most puppies are born with roundworms. These are typically tested for and treated at ages two, four, six, and eight weeks. Your breeder should supply the dates and the kind of medicine used.

Depending on the age of your puppy, he may or may not have received his first set of vaccinations. Currently, many veterinarians give the first set of shots at 8 weeks, then 12 weeks, 16 weeks, and then annually after that, although some veterinarians may also recommend shots at 18 to 20 weeks, and then annually. Check with the breeder to see what, if any, shots have been given to your puppy.

Usually, the shots given are combination vaccinations that include protection against distemper, leptospirosis, hepatitis, parvovirus, and may or may not also include parainfluenza.

Also talk to your veterinarian about the effects of vaccinations, and about whether or not annual vaccinations are needed. After your first vaccination, stay at the veterinarian's office for a while to see if your Dachshund is going to have a reaction. If he does, the medical staff will be

An inoculation against rabies is required in every state, but the timespan between shots may differ. Some states require a rabies shot every year, some every three years. Check with your veterinarian for your state's requirements.

available to quickly counteract the reaction.

If your dog does react to vaccinations, make sure to notify your veterinarian. If he knows this, he might break up the shots for your dog, instead of giving a combination shot, or he might give the general vaccination at one appointment and the rabies shot at another. Splitting up the doses doesn't mean your veterinarian is just trying to get more money from you. It means he is concerned about your dog. Many veterinarians no longer routinely give the Leptospirosis vaccine. Ask your veterinarian about this.

MODERN VACCINE PROTOCOL

The practice of giving every dog every kind of vaccination every year has been challenged in recent years, so that is another thing to talk to your veterinarian about. Tests have shown that almost three-quarters of tested dogs still have a high blood titer against the disease they were vaccinated for, but a high titer doesn't guarantee that they will in fact fight off a disease.

Rather than automatically vaccinating every dog every year, many veterinarians now vaccinate on a case-by-case basis. They might vaccinate show dogs or dogs who travel frequently, more often than older, stay-at-home dogs.

Currently, drug companies are working on longer-lasting

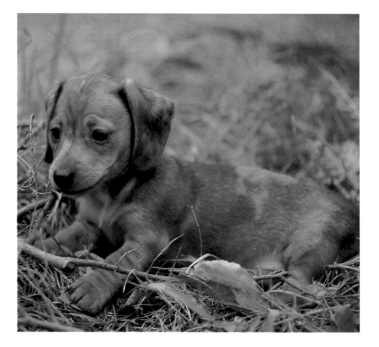

Discuss the important and necessary vaccines your Dachshund will need as a puppy and an adult.

vaccinations; ones that would protect for three to four years. Ask your veterinarian about this, as these should soon be available.

Diseases to be Vaccinated Against

What exactly are the diseases that your dog will be vaccinated against? Let's start with rabies.

Rabies

Rabies is a virus that attacks the central nervous system of mammals and is spread through saliva. Common carriers in the wild include bats, foxes, raccoons, and skunks. Although there have been a few documented cases of survivors, rabies is considered a fatal disease. Once symptoms appear, there is no cure. Rabies can be prevented by vaccinations, which are required by law for dogs.

Distemper

Distemper is another dangerous disease that has a very low recovery rate. The danger from this very contagious virus is greatest in dogs three to six months of age and in dogs over six years of age. Symptoms include vomiting, diarrhea, coughing, and fever, and death is the usual outcome.

Parvovirus

Parvovirus is another disease that may be fatal, especially if the symptoms include vomiting and bloody diarrhea. There may be a fever, and the dog will be lethargic and depressed. Dogs with mild cases of the disease generally recover, but young puppies are very susceptible and generally do not survive. This is why those early shots are so important.

Coronavirus

Coronavirus is a highly contagious virus that results in diarrhea for about a week. The diarrhea may be orange-tinged and will have a strong odor. The disease is rarely fatal, but the dog may need to be treated for dehydration. Talk to your veterinarian about the need for this shot. A healthy, mostly indoor dog might not need this shot, but it might be advisable for a show dog, or a dog that regularly comes in contact with many other dogs. Since it is rarely fatal, you might want to just take your chances.

Canine Hepatitis

Dogs with mild to moderate cases of infectious canine hepatitis generally have a fever and are lethargic. They may

Never give your dog alcoholic beverages. A drunken dog is not funny; a drunken dog is sick, and it doesn't take much to result in alcohol poisoning, which could lead to death.

be reluctant to move and have abdominal tenderness and pale mucous membranes. The mucous membranes may be bright red, yellow, pale, or have petechiation (small red spots/bruising) depending on the stage or course of the disease. An infected dog can recover anywhere from one to five days after showing symptoms, or the disease may progress to death. In dogs with severe cases, the dog may vomit, have diarrhea, and develop a cough. Sudden death may result. The disease is spread through the virus in feces and urine.

Leptospirosis

Leptospirosis is a bacteria frequently transmitted through urine, especially that of rats and mice. Symptoms include vomiting, fever, and a reluctance to move. There may also be signs of renal failure. Severe cases can be fatal. If you live in an area where your dog will be exposed to the urine of rats and mice, you might want to make sure your dog is protected against leptospirosis. Otherwise, this may be a shot you can skip. Consult with your veterinarian.

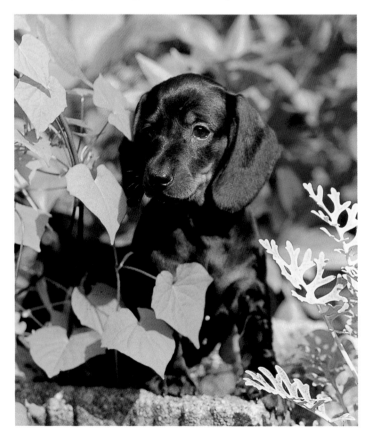

Dogs who spend any amount of time outdoors are liable to pick up fleas and ticks. Preventive care is a must to keep these parasites under control.

Other Important Vaccines
Lyme Disease

The deer tick spreads Lyme disease, and symptoms include lethargy, loss of appetite, and lameness. It is treated with antibiotics. Ask your vet if this disease is a problem in your area.

Bordetella

Vaccination recommendations will depend on where you live, or what you're doing with your dog. Most boarding kennels require a bordetella, or kennel cough vaccination, and that's a good idea if you're traveling a lot, or showing, as kennel cough is highly contagious. Keep in mind that even with a bordetella shot, your dog may still catch kennel cough. There are many varieties, and the vaccine only protects against a few of those. Kennel cough can be treated with antibiotics, and while any disease is cause for concern, kennel cough is not usually serious.

The trend now is away from giving every dog every shot, just because the vaccine is available. Some people will even have a blood test done to see if the dog really needs an annual booster. Talk to your veterinarian about what is best for your Dachshund.

EXTERNAL PARASITES
Fleas

Depending on where you live and the time of year you get your puppy, you may already have encountered fleas or ticks. The flea generally seen in and around dogs is a cat flea and is not native to this continent, but actually came from Africa. It is getting resistant to many of the flea control products on the market today. Fleas are nasty little critters, and if your dog happens to be allergic to flea saliva, they can make your pet miserable.

Combing your dog with a flea comb will also help trap the unwanted guests. A friend of mine combs her dog at the door whenever he comes inside and has had success in keeping down the flea population.

Many Dachshunds seem to be especially sensitive to fleabites. Be aggressive in flea control. If you live in northern areas where winter is a definite season, with lots of cold, you'll have a short break. If you live in a hot, dry area, you may not have any problem at all because it will be too dry for fleas. If you live in a warmer, wetter climate, you'll be facing a year-round battle.

If your dog is scratching and you suspect fleas, turn him over and inspect his stomach, especially toward the back legs

Allergic Reactions

When you're checking your dog for external parasites, pay attention to his skin also. Dogs can be allergic to foods, molds, and pollens, just like people. Usually, these allergies cause itchy skin. If the discomfort is seasonal, it's probably "something in the air." If it's continuous, it could be the food. If your dog's reaction is not too severe, you may have the time to try different foods, such as foods with rice as the basic grain instead of corn or wheat. If there's a severe reaction, once again, you'll need a trip to the veterinarian. He may want to run some tests or he may suggest a food made of all one product. These special diets have just one ingredient, such as duck, and then, by gradually adding other foods, you can eventually determine the exact cause of the allergy. It's a lengthy process and fortunately, most dogs don't need to go this route.

If your dog is allergic to flea saliva, he will bite and scratch where a flea has bitten and may do damage to himself if the irritation drives him to continuous biting and scratching at one spot. Whether or not he is allergic, if he is licking or biting at an area, for whatever reason, that area can develop into a hot spot. Hot spots are raw, red, oozy-looking spots that can spread and get infected if not treated. I use a triple antibiotic salve on hot spots, and this seems to clear them up. If a hot spot doesn't get better or continues to get larger, check with your veterinarian.

where the fur is thinner. Push the hair against the grain. You may see a flea or two scurrying for cover. Or, you may not see a flea at all, but you may notice flecks of flea dirt. If you're not sure if what you're looking at is flea dirt, or just regular dirt, collect a bit on a white piece of paper or paper towel, and wet it. If it turns reddish, it's flea dirt.

If you don't see anything on your dog but still suspect fleas, run a flea comb through your dog's coat. Flea combs have very fine, closely set teeth that can trap fleas. Once you've determined that there are fleas, the war has begun.

Start with the dog. There are many different products on the market, and your veterinarian can help you choose the one best suited for your dog. If your dog is heavily infested, a bath using a flea-fighting shampoo is a good idea first.

Ticks

Ticks may or may not be a problem in your area. If you take long walks in tall grass or through brush, you are more likely to pick up a tick or two than in a backyard. Deer ticks, which are very small, can spread Lyme disease. Ask your vet if this is a concern in your area, as there is a vaccine for Lyme disease.

You can remove ticks gently with tweezers, or put alcohol on them. Never use a cigarette or anything else that will burn. Undoubtedly that would get the tick's attention, but you are also apt to burn your dog. If you don't think you can get the tick off properly, or just don't want to try, have your veterinarian do it for you. The important thing is to check your dog on a routine basis if ticks are a problem in your area and not leave them on your dog. Ticks can be hard to find, so be patient and thorough.

Mites

Mites can cause mange, another skin problem to watch out for. There are two types of mange, both caused by tiny mites. With sarcoptic mange, there is intense itching, and with advanced cases, skin lesions and hair loss. It is treated with ivermectin internally and externally with sulfur dips. Treatment usually lasts for three weeks. The dog's bedding should be thoroughly disinfected or thrown away.

Demodectic mange is passed from the mother to the puppies and affects puppies between the ages of three and ten months. With demodectic mange, you may notice hair loss around the eyes, lips, or on the forelegs. The dog may also lose hair at the tips of the ears. Demodectic mange doesn't cause the itching that sarcoptic mange does and it is usually diagnosed from skin scrapings. A special shampoo may be recommended and ivermectin is again used. Demodectic mange, if not widespread on the dog's body, may go away on its own. If it spreads beyond small, localized areas, it may need up to a year of treatment.

Internal Parasites (Worms)

Internal parasites can be harder to detect than those living on the surface, and that's why a fecal check once or twice a year is so important. Whipworms, hookworms, and roundworms can all be discovered by a fecal check. Heartworms require a blood test, and tapeworm segments are usually evident in the stool and can be seen with the naked eye.

Tapeworms

Tapeworms are the least harmful of the worms that may infest your dog. Your Dachshund can acquire tapeworms from swallowing a flea, so controlling the flea population is one of the best ways to prevent tapeworms in your dog. Tapeworm segments are visible in the stool and will look like small grains of rice. Check your dog's stool periodically for evidence of tapeworms.

Hookworm

Hookworm eggs are passed in the feces and can live in the soil. They may also be passed from a bitch to her puppies. Instead of maturing, larvae may live in the bitch and then pass to the puppies through the mammary glands. Hookworms feed on the blood of their host and can cause fatal anemia in puppies.

Roundworms

Roundworms are the most common worms that can affect your dog. They contaminate the soil and the eggs are very resistant to adverse conditions. They are able to remain in the soil for years. Most puppies are born with these worms because the larvae are able to live in an intermediate host, in this case the bitch, but not infect her. This is why it is necessary to worm young puppies.

Whipworms

Whipworms can cause deep inflammation of the colon. If your dog has periodic bouts of diarrhea with mucus and blood, he may have whipworms. Again, contaminated soil is to blame. Protect your dog from worms with periodic fecal checks and use the medicine your veterinarian prescribes to get rid of them.

Heartworm

Heartworm is a deadly parasite that does not show up in fecal checks, but requires a blood test to detect. This parasite can kill or incapacitate your dog, and the cure can be almost as bad as the disease. It is much better to prevent it than cure it. Heartworm larvae develop in mosquitoes and are passed to the dog when a mosquito bites him. These larvae move to the chambers of the right side of the dog's heart. There the worms mature and produce microfilariae, which circulate in the blood until another mosquito ingests them after feeding on the dog. Adult heartworms can completely fill the heart chambers. An infected dog may tire easily and develop a cough.

An annual blood test can tell whether any microfilariae are present. Talk to your veterinarian about a monthly heartworm preventative for your dog. Some prevent only heartworms; some also include chemicals that kill other worms, such as hookworms.

Puppies can get worms from their mother's milk, something that is easily remedied as long as you take your puppy for his first vet checkup promptly.

If your dog does get heartworms, the first step is to get rid of the adult worms. In the past, heartworms were usually treated with a series of injections of an arsenical drug that was administered intravenously (thiacetarsamide sodium). This treatment sometimes had serious side effects. Now, the infestation is more commonly treated with a newer medication, melarsomine dihydrochloride, which is given intramuscularly into the lumbar muscles. This is generally a much safer treatment with fewer side effects.

The worms die slowly and are carried to the lungs by the blood stream, where they gradually disintegrate. Enforced rest for four to six weeks following treatment is very important for full recovery. If the pet is allowed to be too active, fatal emboli may occur that can result in permanent damage or death.

DISEASES COMMON TO DACHSHUNDS

There are some diseases and conditions that are common with Dachshunds.

Eye Problems

You already know that they can have eye problems because of their position.

Dachshunds may also be susceptible to entropion, which is where the eyelashes grow inward, scratching the eye. This can be corrected by surgery.

Trichiasis is a similar problem where otherwise normal eyelashes turn inward, irritating the cornea. Again, surgery is possible to correct the problem.

Progressive Retinal Atrophy (PRA) is another eye condition affecting Dachshunds that can lead to blindness. Ask your breeder if she tests her breeding stock for this disease. PRA generally strikes older dogs and results in gradual blindness. A dog with PRA will start to have trouble seeing at night first. There is no treatment, and a dog with PRA will eventually be totally blind.

Back Problems

Dachshunds are prone to intervertebral disk degeneration, which is a degeneration of the cushioning disks between the vertebrae of the spinal cord. When a disk ruptures, this puts pressure on the nerves and can result in pain and/or lameness or paralysis. While jumping will not cause the problem, it may aggravate it. Keeping your dog at a proper weight and in good muscle tone will help. If a disk does rupture, anti-inflammatories and rest may be enough to get your dog back to normal. In severe cases, surgery may be required.

Your Dachshund may also injure a disk by just "being a dog." Dachshunds are bold little dogs and may think nothing of launching from the sofa or your bed. It's up to you to make sure your Dachshund doesn't do this. Lift your Dachshund down from the furniture. Yes, he's willing to jump down, but with those short legs and that long back, he could injure himself. Pay attention to how you pick up your dog as well, and don't let his hindquarters dangle in space. Make sure you support the entire dog when you lift or carry him. Playing Frisbee with your Dachshund is probably not a good idea either, because leaping and twisting can result in a back injury. Just throw a ball and let him run straight after it. Again, keeping your dog at the right weight will help prevent back strain. The more your dog weighs, the harder it

Because they stand low to the ground, a Dachshund's eyes are more vulnerable to dirt, dust, grass, and other irritants.

is on his skeleton.

Spondylosis deformans is a degenerative condition of the spine. Bony spurs form around the edges of the vertebral end plates, and these spurs may bridge, or almost bridge, the disk spaces. The condition causes stiffness and back pain, and the dog may also be lame. X-rays will determine if this is the problem, and a veterinarian will generally prescribe nonsteroidal anti-inflammatory drugs to treat the pain.

The Dachshund's long spine and short legs make him prone to intervertebral disk degeneration. Your veterinarian should know to check his spine for this problem.

Epilepsy

Epilepsy is another condition that can affect Dachshunds, and currently there is no way to genetically test for this problem. In many cases, the seizures can be controlled with medication.

A seizure may or may not be epilepsy. To be defined as epilepsy, many veterinarians say there needs to be recurrent seizures with no other disease detected. Sometimes a dog will have an isolated seizure and never have another one. Although the seizure itself is not likely to hurt the dog, unless he bumps into something or falls against something, watching a seizure can be frightening. Be calm until the seizure is over and then call your veterinarian for his advice. Most likely he'll ask you to describe the seizure and tell you to keep watching your dog. If it makes you feel better, ask for an appointment for a checkup for your dog.

Watching Your Dog's Weight After Being Fixed

There shouldn't be much weight gain in a spayed or neutered animal if their exercise level doesn't change. None of my females ever gained any weight after being spayed, but my male did, in fact, gain a bit. Cutting his food from a cup a day to three-quarters of a cup a day brought him back to his ideal weight.

In a seizure, a dog may have muscle spasms, may paddle with his legs, salivate, urinate, defecate, vomit, or any combination of these things. A dog having a partial seizure may try to crawl to you. Reassurance and love may shorten the seizure. Do be careful, though, if your dog is having a seizure, because sometimes dogs having a seizure may snap or bite.

There is currently no way to genetically test for epilepsy, and if your dog only has the occasional seizure, there will likely be no treatment. If seizures are frequent, your veterinarian may prescribe an anticonvulsant. Acupuncture may also be useful in controlling seizures.

Teeth and Gum Problems

The teeth are easy to ignore, but teeth and gum problems can lead to more serious problems as bacteria are produced and circulated throughout the dog. See Chapter 5 to learn ways to brush your dog's teeth and help prevent dental problems. If you suspect a problem, have your veterinarian examine your Dachshund's teeth.

Raising puppies is expensive and time consuming, and unless you plan for them very carefully, it's best to spay or neuter your dogs and leave the breeding to professionals.

Obesity

Obesity shouldn't be a problem in dogs because they have people to control their food intake. Unfortunately, it's all too easy to give in to those pleading eyes and slip the dog a piece of cheese or the leftover pizza crust. And sometimes people think kibble looks unappealing and adding a bit of meat and gravy will make it taste better. Or, while training our dog we forget that all those food rewards also add calories.

For whatever reason, once a dog gets fat, the extra weight affects his health. Added weight can lead to added stress on that long spine. Added weight can also lead to heart problems and may lead to diabetes. A fat dog has trouble exercising, so he may gain even more weight.

If you can't feel your dog's ribs when you run your hands over his sides, he's too fat.

A dog's normal temperature is between 100° and 102°F, with a heart rate of 80 to 140 beats per minute. If the temperature goes above 104°, or below 100°F, call the veterinarian. If the dog is bleeding and the blood is spurting, or can't be stopped by pressure, call the veterinarian.

Hyperthyroidism

Hyperthyroidism in dogs is usually caused by a tumor on the thyroid. Symptoms include weight loss, increased appetite, heat intolerance, restless behavior, frequent defecation with only partially formed stools, increased drinking and increased urinating. Treatment is surgery, and, if the tumor is cancerous and has spread, radioiodine and chemotherapy.

Hypothyroidism

Dachshunds are one of the breeds at increased risk for hypothyroidism. The problem is usually seen between 4 and 10 years of age. Symptoms include hair loss, usually at the base of the tail, ears and lower back, a dry coat, and flaky, oily skin. The dog may be lethargic, be more sensitive to cold and

Emergency Poison Hotlines

If you suspect poisoning, don't wait! Call the vet to let her know you're on the way. If this is not possible, call the ASPCA National Animal Poison Control Center at 1-800-548-2423. Have your credit card ready as there is a consulting fee. Or, call 1-900-680-0000 and the charges will be added to your phone bill. If you know what your dog ate, you can induce vomiting by administering hydrogen peroxide, but don't encourage vomiting if the substance is unknown. Caustic products, such as many household cleaners, will cause more damage when the dog vomits. Give the dog lots of milk or vegetable oil.

may gain weight. In severe cases there may be muscle weakness. Treatment is with a replacement hormone, which may be administered as a pill, or by injection or IV.

Diabetes

Diabetes is another disease frequently seen in Dachshunds. The onset of the disease is usually between 4 and 14 years, with the peak between between 7 and 9 years. Females are more likely to get diabetes than males. Increased drinking and urinating are the most obvious symptoms. In fact, diabetes is commonly diagnosed when a previously housetrained dog starts having accidents in the house. You may notice acetone on your dog's breath; it smells like nail polish remover. In advanced cases of diabetes the dog may be lethargic, be dehydrated, may be vomiting, and may have diarrhea. Treatment is injections of insulin.

Cancer

Cancer is one of the scariest words in the English language, but many cancers, if caught in time, can be treated. Some are more treatable than others, which is why you should never wait if you suspect a problem. Many surface tumors, for example, are easily removed when they are small. Testicular cancer is another form that is usually treated successfully. Some cancers may respond to chemotherapy or radiation treatments and if they cannot be cured, at least they may be put into remission, giving you more time with your Dachshund.

Groom your dog regularly, and make it a habit to run your hands over his body so that you notice any unusual lump or bump or sore. If the injury doesn't get better or a lump is growing, make that appointment with your veterinarian. Don't wait for the possibility that the cancer will spread.

SPAYING AND NEUTERING

Between six months and two years of age, besides finishing off the growth period, your dog will become sexually mature. Spaying or neutering can eliminate some of the manifestations of sexual maturity, and certainly this is the best approach if you are not seriously committed to showing or breeding.

As your male matures, he will start "lifting his leg" more and more frequently on walks, marking his territory, and announcing his presence to other dogs. He may start marking in the house as well, which can be a very hard habit to break. He may or may not become more aggressive toward other males. He will certainly become more interested in females. If he is around a female in season, he will pay less attention, if any, to you. If he were to ever get loose, he would be more apt to stray farther from home than a neutered male.

If you have a female, you can expect her to come in season sometime between six months and a year of age, and then every six to eight months after that. Ask your breeder what the females are like in her line, as there can be some

Common Toxins Indoors and Out

Sharing a fenced yard with your Dachshund is much more fun than just taking him for walks, but remember, there can be dangers in your own backyard. Tomato plant stems and leaves and rhubarb leaves are poisonous. Ask your veterinarian or the people at the greenhouse which plants might be toxic to a dog. This doesn't mean that you can't have a garden as well as a dog. For instance, the bulbs of many plants are poisonous, but even if your Dachshund has a passion for digging, a small fence can protect both the flowers and your dog.

variation. A bitch is in season for about 21 days, although she is only receptive to a male for 3 to 5 of those days.

The amount of discharge can vary, and how clean the bitch is can also make a difference in how much cleaning up you do. You may want to confine your dog to a room without carpeting while she is in season. If you have a fenced yard and plan to put her out unattended, make sure the fence is solid and is high enough to prevent any wandering males from jumping in. Keep an eye on her. Don't just put her out and forget her. If you are walking her, keep a good grip on the lead and keep your eye out for romantic males. If you own more than one dog and one is an intact male, you just might want to board the bitch, rather than deal with trying to keep her separated from the male in the house. Males can be very persistent and frequently vocal, and three weeks can be a long time.

Besides the benefits of no unwanted litters, spaying a female before her first heat lowers the chance of mammary tumors. After the first heat, there is not much difference in the incidence of these tumors, but spaying does end the chance of pyometra and other reproductive infections as well as the twice-yearly "season." Intact males may be susceptible to prostatic hypertrophy, which is a benign enlargement of the prostate. Neutering prevents prostate problems and may curb aggression and end marking in the house.

On this last point, if you have had a male who persists in lifting his leg against any and all furniture, it is a real relief when he stops. I showed my male until he was about four, and then considered neutering, but was told that at his age, his behavior patterns were set and neutering would probably not change his habit of marking. I left him alone, going through rolls and rolls of paper towels and bottles and bottles of white vinegar. Then I decided to purchase a puppy bitch to show. I wanted no accidental litters and didn't want the hassle of keeping them separated or boarding one or the other when the bitch came in season. Griffin was neutered. He hasn't marked since. This might not be true for everyone, but it is definitely worth a try.

CONSIDERING BREEDING

If you bought your puppy as a pet, the breeder probably gave you a limited registration and may have made spaying or neutering a requirement of the purchase. If, however, the breeder sees promise in the dog and agrees that the quality is there for breeding, be aware that breeding is not something to be undertaken lightly. For starters, there's the stud fee and the cost of shipping your bitch to the male. If you decide on chilled or frozen semen, there's expense involved in gathering, shipping, and inseminating. With these last methods, you'll need daily testing to determine when your female is ready to be bred. There'll be testing for brucellosis, as well as for any hereditary problems. There's the cost of an ultrasound to determine the number of puppies. You'll need to buy or build a whelping box. The female may need a caesarian section. Some or all of the puppies could die of various causes. The mother could die, leaving you with an orphan litter to feed and clean every two hours. If no one wants the puppies, they'll be your responsibility until you do find them a home, and that means vaccinations, worming, crate training, and the beginning of housetraining.

Breeding is not for the faint of heart. If you are not seriously committed to raising and breeding Dachshunds, and just want another pet, go back to your breeder and buy another one. It will be a lot less work and you'll be much happier.

FIRST AID FOR YOUR DACHSHUND

Dachshunds are generally healthy, but there are things to watch for in any dog. Any problem that persists longer than 24 hours is reason to call your vet. Also, any problem that worsens over several hours, or produces loss of appetite, weakness, or fever needs prompt medical attention. If your dog has a mild case of diarrhea or vomits once or twice, stop all food for a day and give only water for 24 hours. You may want to feed cooked ground meat with rice for a day or two

Almost everyone knows that antifreeze can be deadly, and you'd never let your dog drink bleach, but furniture polish, shoe polish, boric acid, deodorants, detergents, and disinfectants are also harmful and should be kept away from your dog.

afterward. If there are frequent bouts of vomiting or diarrhea, or if it continues for more than 24 hours, call the veterinarian.

There are probably hundreds of products that may be considered poisonous to your dog, but many can be avoided just by using common sense, and many products will probably never be ingested in large enough amounts to harm your pet. For instance, apple seeds contain cyanide. The odds are against your Dachshund ever eating massive quantities of apple seeds. If you are sharing your apple with your Dachshund and he eats a seed or two, don't panic. He should be fine.

The following first-aid information might make you think twice about even having a dog, but with luck, you won't ever have to worry about any of the problems described below. It's just good to know that there are first-aid measures you can take to help your pet if something ever does happen. Many local Red Cross branches offer animal first-aid courses, which can help you understand just what you can do to help your pet until you can reach the veterinarian.

Taking Your Dog's Pulse

First, learn to take your dog's pulse. The femoral artery is probably the easiest to find. It's on the upper rear leg, near where the leg joins the body. Find the top bone of the rear leg, which is the femur. Move forward just a bit and you should be able to feel the artery. You might want to ask your vet to help you find it the first time. Find it before you need it, when you and the dog are both calm. Then, when there's an emergency, you'll be able to find it quickly without panicking.

The normal pulse rate for a dog is between 80 to 140 beats per minute, and the smaller the dog, the higher the number. If you're having your veterinarian show you how to take your dog's pulse, see what your dog's normal range is at the same time, then if there's a problem you'll have a number to use for comparison.

Choking

If your dog is choking on something, use the handle of a screwdriver between the back teeth to keep his mouth open and prevent the dog from biting as you check out his throat and mouth. If you can see the object causing the problem, use your fingers, or a pair of needle-nosed pliers to remove it. If you can't reach it, hold your dog upside down by the hind legs and shake him. If that doesn't work, apply forceful, sudden pressure to the abdomen at the edge of the breastbone. (Use your fist. Think Heimlich maneuver.)

Staying Calm in an Emergency

In case of a major emergency, such as a dogfight, or if your dog is hit by a car, it is natural to panic, but you need to stay calm for the sake of your dog. In spite of the voice in your head telling you to hurry, slow down and take a moment to think about what your best course of action should be. All too often, improper handling on the spur of the moment can result in further injury to the dog and possibly injury to you.

When a dog is hurt, frightened, or in pain, he is apt to snap blindly at any touch, even yours. A muzzle will protect you and make it easier to treat and transport your dog. You might consider buying a nylon muzzle from a pet supply store or catalog, or you can use a length of gauze from the roll in the first-aid kit.

The best way to transport an injured animal is on a blanket or a board, especially if any spinal cord injury is suspected. Get help, if possible, and try to shift the dog all at once to the blanket or board. Try to move him as little as possible. Call your veterinarian. Give him a brief description of your dog's injuries and tell him you are on the way. Although you may feel calling the doctor's office is wasting time, your call gives the staff the time they need to prepare for the emergency. Take the time to call ahead.

Injury Checklist

When your dog has been injured, there may be cuts and lacerations. These may produce a lot of blood and look messy, but they are probably the least of your concerns.

In order of importance, check:

1. Airway/Breathing: Is the air passage clear? Is breathing labored?
2. Circulation: Is the dog in shock? Is there significant blood loss?
3. Neurologic: Has a head, neck or back injury likely occurred?
4. Orthopedic: Do you suspect broken bones?

Buffered aspirin is an appropriate pain or fever reducer at the correct dosage, but alternatives such as Tylenol, Motrin, Advil, and so on are not. They are poisonous to your dog.

If something is lodged in your dog's mouth, you may need a flashlight to get a better look.

5. Ocular: Do you suspect or detect any significant eye injuries?

Report your findings or suspicions to your veterinarian when you call.

Administering CPR

Make sure there's nothing in your dog's mouth, nose, or throat that is choking him or blocking the airway. If he isn't breathing, you'll need to perform artificial respiration. If you've rescued your Dachshund from a pool, hold him upside down by his hind legs for about 30 seconds to allow fluid to drain from his lungs and mouth before you attempt artificial respiration.

Otherwise, place your dog on his side with his neck extended. Hold the dog's muzzle closed and place your mouth over the dog's nose. Slowly blow air into the dog's nose so that his chest expands. You may also

Rehydrating Your Dog

If your dog has been vomiting or has had diarrhea, he may be dehydrated. Your veterinarian may suggest Gatorade or Pediolyte. My experience is that your dog won't like either one. Try them, but don't be surprised if your dog turns up his nose at both. My dogs will eat ice cubes in any weather, so I give those. Chicken or beef bouillon may also tempt them, and the salty taste may encourage them to head for the water bowl as well. Water drained from a can of tuna may flavor a bowl of water enough to encourage your dog to drink.

have to administer CPR (Cardio-Pulmonary Resuscitation). Place your dog on his left side and place your thumb on one side of the chest and your fingers on the other side. Compress the chest by squeezing. Do 100 compressions per minute, stopping every 30 seconds to see if the dog is breathing on his own.

Signs of Shock

Now, what about circulation? Is your dog in shock? If your dog has been in a serious fight or has been hit by a car, chances are he'll be in shock. Check the color of his gums, lips and eyelids. If they are pale, that's a sign of shock. He may feel cool to the touch, especially his legs. See if his temperature is down. His breathing may be shallow and irregular. Check his pulse. It may be fast, irregular and faint. Wrap him in a blanket, or, if you don't have one, a jacket or coat, or even newspapers, anything to keep him warm. Do not use a heat lamp or anything hot close to the body. Because he will likely be unconscious and his circulation will be poor, this could result in burns. Keep him in a horizontal position. A Boy Scout I knew learned a handy phrase in his first-aid course that can also be applied to dogs, "If the head is pale, elevate the tail." There's no need for a huge elevation of the hindquarters, but at least maintain the horizontal position.

Has there been significant blood loss? If so, try to find any external wounds that may need a pressure bandage. If you don't have a bandage, use a towel, or if necessary, your hand. A tourniquet on a leg should only be used as a last resort. A tourniquet stops the blood, which means that all the tissue below the tourniquet will start to die. Use a tourniquet only if you are sure that without it your pet will die. Tighten it only enough to stop the bleeding and get your dog to the veterinarian immediately.

If your Dachshund has suffered a head, back, or neck injury, try not to move him any more than necessary. Slide him onto a board, a piece of cardboard, or a blanket all at once. Use gauze strips to hold him in place and again, get to your veterinarian.

Do you suspect broken bones? There are all kinds of materials you can use to make a splint for a broken leg. Just remember that the splint should extend beyond the joints

Generally, a visit to the veterinarian is indicated with any problem (vomiting, diarrhea, fever, lack of appetite, weakness) that lasts 24 hours or more. The longer you have your Dachshund, the better you'll be able to tell whether a stomach upset just requires some rest and a bland diet to correct it, or whether you need the veterinarian. When in doubt, make the appointment. You'll feel better knowing just what the problem is, and when it comes to your Dachshund's health, it really is better to be safe than sorry.

Acupuncture can be particularly helpful for easing pain and promoting healing commonly associated with serious medical issues.

on either side of the break. Protect the leg with some padding if you are using sticks or pieces of wood as a splint. Or, you can use a magazine or newspaper for the splint, tying it on with gauze or using vet wrap, or even a nylon or a knee sock. If pieces of bone are protruding, don't try to push them back. Cover with a gauze pad and stabilize the area as well as possible.

If there's a puncture wound or other type of injury that penetrates into the chest cavity, try to make it airtight with bandages or plastic wrap. You want it airtight, but not so tight as to hinder breathing. If whatever made the wound is still in it, leave it there for your veterinarian to remove. Use bandages to stabilize the object, if necessary, so it doesn't do any more damage.

Did your Dachshund's eyes escape injury? If the eyelid is bleeding, you may use a gauze pad and gently hold it in place, but remember the word *gently*. Too much pressure could cause even more damage. If the blood is inside the eyeball, just get to the veterinarian and don't attempt anything yourself. If your Dachshund's eye has actually popped out of the socket, keep it moist and get to the veterinarian immediately. Use artificial tears, contact lens solution, plain water, cod liver oil, or olive oil. Applying the moisturizer every 15 or 20 minutes should be enough.

If you want to learn more about acupuncture, or want to find a veterinarian in your area who practices acupuncture, www.ivas.org is the web site for the International Veterinary Acupuncture Society. It lists certified veterinary acupuncturists by state in the US, and by country around the world.

With time and practice, you will not panic over minor problems, but will learn when you can wait and when you need to make an emergency visit to the veterinarian's office. When in doubt, always call your veterinarian. He can offer the help and reassurance you need. I'd rather pay for an unnecessary office visit than ignore something and be sorry later.

A First-Aid Kit

Whether you have a separate first-aid kit for your dog, or just keep supplies in a bathroom drawer, there are some basic items you should have on hand in case of emergencies. If you travel frequently with your dog, keep a box of the basics in your car, too. Label the boxes expressly for this purpose, and check the expiration dates on the products occasionally to be sure they're active.

- Syrup of ipecac—give by mouth to induce vomiting
- Activated charcoal—give by mouth if your dog has swalowed something poisonous
- Hydrogen peroxide—to cleanse wounds; this can also induce vomiting
- Gauze rolls or pads
- Adhesive tape
- Cotton balls
- Safety scissors
- Artificial tears—for eye irritation
- Hemostats and/or tweezers
- Digital thermometer
- Syringes (3, 6, and 12 cc)—to administer medication
- Children's Benadryl—for allergic reactions, give 1 milligram per pound
- Children's aspirin or buffered asprin—for fever or pain. Give one tablet per 10 to 15 pounds of body weight.
- Antibiotic ointment—topical for infected wounds
- Hydrocortisone ointment—topical for bug bites or rashes
- Index card with your vet's phone number and the number of the local emergency clinic
- A veterinary first-aid manual
- You might also want some rubber gloves and a roll of vet wrap. This is good for holding bandages or splints in place and it doesn't stick to your dog's fur.

Aloe vera can provide temporary relief for hot spots, bites, and many other skin irritations. Besides being nontoxic, aloe vera is also bitter so it may discourage licking, which can slow healing.

If Your Dog Is Lost

No matter what method or methods you use for identification, if your dog should become lost, don't rely on tags, tattoos, or microchips to get your dog back. Be aggressive. Make up posters of your dog. If you have a scanner, a printer, and a computer, you can make your own posters, complete with picture. Otherwise, have the local copy shop make them for you. A sharp black and white image may be better than a color picture that doesn't clearly show your dog. Keep a good photo of your dog on hand in case of emergency. Try to get a picture that shows the dog clearly. Your Dachshund may look adorable curled up in a ball amongst the sofa cushions, but will that adorable pose help to bring him home? The next time you have the camera out for a holiday or birthday, take a few snaps of your dog. If you have a black Dachshund, try to take a picture of him against a light background. If your Dachshund is red, find a dark background.

Lost Dog To-Do List

- Take the best picture you have and put it on the poster, along with your phone number. Mention the general area where the dog was lost—for instance, in the vicinity of Green Park, or between Maple and Elm Streets. State the dog's sex. Mention age. It may be more helpful to say "puppy" or "older dog with gray muzzle" than to say a specific age. If the dog is wearing a collar, mention that, as well as the collar's color. If your photo is in black and white, list the color or colors of your dog. If your Dachshund is red, you might want to say "brown" on the poster. Remember, not everyone knows that the official name of the Dachshund's color is red. Offer a reward, but don't specify the amount on the poster.
- Go door to door and ask your immediate neighbors to keep an eye out for your dog. Leave them a poster. Put posters on area bulletin boards, in veterinarian's offices, and at local stores. Recruit children. They probably cover more territory on foot than the adults in your neighborhood, and they may be more apt to notice a dog. Don't encourage children to actually try to catch your dog. Ask them to come to you and lead you to the dog, or to tell their parents and have them call you. A lost dog is frequently a frightened dog, and you don't want him chased farther away. You also don't want to run the risk of your dog biting someone out of fear.
- Call area veterinary hospitals. There's a chance your dog could have been hit by a car and taken to a veterinarian. Call again.
- Check with your local animal shelter. Go in person and look at the dogs. Don't rely on phone calls, and don't rely on having someone at a shelter call you. Leave your name and phone number, of course, but also check in person. Notes can be lost, and shelter personnel may change. The person you talk to may not know what a Dachshund is, especially if you have a Wirehair or a Longhair. They may have seen your dog and thought he was a mixed breed. Go look at the dogs who have been picked up as strays. Go look at least every other day. Show the staff pictures of your dog.
- If there's another shelter 20 or 30 miles away, visit it, too. Dogs, even Dachshunds, can travel amazing distances. Also, if someone picked up your dog and dropped him off again, or lost him, he could end up farther away.
- Run an ad in the Lost and Found column of your local newspaper. Ask your area radio stations to announce it. Many newspapers and radio stations are happy to run these kinds of public service announcements at no charge.
- Notify your breeder. Check with Dachshund rescue. Other Dachshund people can be a helpful resource and if they see a stray Dachshund can help you get him back. If your area has a local kennel club, let them know, too. Dog people are generally eager to help other dog people, and they may be more likely to know what a coated Dachshund looks like.

Having clear pictures of your dog that you can make into flyers or posters will help people recognize your dog if he gets lost.

Holistic First-Aid Kit

Should you want to have some alternatives around to handle common problems and emergencies, here are some suggestions from holistic veterinarian Jean Hofve, DVM:

- Cayenne pepper—apply to wounds to help stop bleeding
- Calendula gel—topical for wound healing
- Arnica gel—topical for sprains, strains, bruises
- Comfrey ointment—topical for wound healing
- Rescue Remedy—the Bach Flower remedy all-purpose liquid that's effective for stress or shock

GIVING YOUR DOG MEDICINE

There may be times when your veterinarian will prescribe some form of medication for your Dachshund. Usually, this will be in pill form. If it's an antibiotic, make sure you give it all, even if your dog seems to be better. You want to make sure that an infection is taken care of and doesn't have a chance to flare up again.

Pills are probably the easiest form of medicine to give a Dachshund. Most Dachshunds are chowhounds. Many will gulp down a pill all by itself, or if it's just lying on top of their food. Otherwise, a bit of food around the pill will make it acceptable. With Dachshunds, this can be just about anything. You can use a spoonful of yogurt, a dab of peanut butter, some cream cheese, a bite of hot dog, some canned dog food, almost anything that your dog will eat quickly, taking the pill with it.

Liquids are a bit harder, unless they have a good flavor and can be mixed with the dog's food. If that doesn't work, pull the dog's lower lip out on the side, making a little pocket into which you can pour the liquid. Then quickly close the dog's mouth and gently stroke his throat until he swallows. Having a helper to hold the dog might be a good idea.

When I've had to put drops and ointment into my dog's eye, I've held him between my legs, and approached the eye from behind. It's not too hard to gently hold open the eye a bit and squeeze in drops or ointment. With ointments, I then close the eye tightly so that the salve will melt and it won't just stick to the eyelashes.

ALTERNATIVE TREATMENTS

More and more veterinary practices are going beyond the bounds of traditional medicine to offer you and your pet as many treatment options as possible. Here are some of them.

Acupuncture

Acupuncture has been practiced on humans in China for more than 4,500 years and on animals for about 2,000 years. Using hair-fine needles, an acupuncturist stimulates appropriate acupoints to help with healing. Acupoints are tiny areas on the skin that contain relatively concentrated levels of nerve endings, lymphatics, and blood vessels. Acupoints can be identified by their lower electrical resistance, and are usually located in small palpable depressions detectable by trained acupuncturists.

Studies have shown that acupuncture can increase blood flow, lower heart rate, and improve immune function. Acupuncture also stimulates the release of certain neurotransmitters like endorphins, the body's natural painkillers, and smaller amounts of cortisol, an anti-inflammatory steroid.

Acupuncture is commonly used for treating chronic

conditions like arthritis and allergies, and to relieve pain and inflammation. Epilepsy may also be helped by acupuncture. Lisa Goldstein, DVM, says that in traditional Chinese medicine acupuncture would be about 20 percent of the treatment, and 80 percent would be herbs, but in this country, people tend to focus more on the acupuncture alone.

Using both acupuncture and herbs, she treated her dog for epilepsy, starting with one treatment a week for three weeks and then once a month for three months, then once every six months, then not at all.

Goldstein says that acupuncture can help speed healing, especially after back surgery. With acupuncture, less pain medicine is needed and the improved blood flow aids healing. She has used it on Dachshunds to help with allergies and skin conditions. Acupuncture can also be used to treat the side effects of cancer, like pain and nausea.

She notes that there are specific "alarm points" that may help indicate what is wrong with an animal. For example, there may be no response when you stimulate the alarm point, but if there is a problem with a specific organ, stimulating the alarm point may provoke a reaction from the animal. A dog may try to bite. Goldstein uses acupuncture to complement Western medicine. She does blood tests and makes her diagnosis based on Western medicine, and then uses the acupuncture to help ease pain and hasten healing. She also encourages her clients to use acupressure points at home in between acupuncture treatments.

Homeopathy

Homeopathy is based on the theory that like heals like. A substance is diluted in several stages so that is it safe and free from side effects, yet is still powerful enough to act as a healing agent. A rough estimate of more than 3,000 homeopathic remedies are in use. These come in tablets, powders, granules, liquids, and ointments. While the idea may be hard to grasp, it becomes a bit clearer when you realize that, as Goldstein points out, vaccines work the same way.

Herbs

At the web site for the International Veterinary Acupuncturist Society many of the doctors listed have TCM after their names, indicating that they practice traditional

Chinese medicine. This may include use of herbs in treatment. Herbal medicines overall may be gentler and safer when properly administered than extracts or synthetic compounds. This does not mean you should dash off to the drugstore and give your dog herbal tablets. Consult with a veterinarian who understands the correct way to use herbs to help heal.

Another aspect of Chinese medicine is the use of certain foods as treatments. An example is using salty foods, such as kelp and seaweed, to soften hardened tissue. This may help with muscle spasms and enlarged lymph glands.

Bach Flower Remedies

Bach flower remedies are often mentioned along with herbal and homeopathic methods. There are 38 single remedies meant to treat emotional problems, such as fear of noise, or shyness. Rescue Remedy, which is a mixture of five of the single remedies, is effective in cases of shock, collapse, and trauma. Many holistic veterinarians will suggest Rescue Remedy as a part of your dog's first-aid kit. Check your local health food store for this product.

Massage

Massage can be a wonderful way to relax your dog, as well as be a pleasant way for the two of you to bond. Linda Tellington-Jones developed the Tellington T-touch method of massage in which repeated massaging movements are said to generate specific brain wave patterns that can help an animal that is suffering from anxiety, especially following injuries or surgery. Healing takes place more rapidly when the animal is calm.

Even if your dog is not suffering from an injury, or any form of anxiety, a massage can sooth tired muscles and can just plain feel good. It's a terrific way to relax your dog and strengthen the bond between the two of you. If what you are doing annoys or hurts your dog, stop doing it! That seems simple, but you may be so sure that your dog is going to enjoy the massage that you may miss him telling you he doesn't. However, massage is no substitute for veterinary care.

Chiropractic

Chiropractic treatment may also help your dog,

especially if you and he are very active. An adjustment may be just what your Dachshund needs to keep zipping around that agility course. Find a veterinarian who not only offers chiropractic services, but will also know if some other form of treatment is needed.

While you may not feel comfortable with every type of alternative or traditional veterinary care, you may come to appreciate a veterinarian who is willing to try all forms of treatment to give the best health care to his patients. So many alternatives are, in fact, complementary to traditional medicine.

YOUR DACHSHUND'S SENIOR YEARS

As your friend ages with you and your family, pay particular attention to his physical and mental needs. Just like us, animals are affected by age in many ways. Not only will you find your Dachshund sleeping more and slowing down a bit overall, you'll notice changes in his coat (more white hairs), changes in his skin (thickening in parts, more droop around the eyes, etc.), changes in his senses, and changes in his temperament. He may be less responsive to your calls or body language, and he may be moodier. These are all changes you should take note of and, if any of them become a real problem, consult your veterinarian.

Otherwise, the kind and responsible thing to do is care for your senior citizen as you would any other member of your family—with some additional "tender loving care," including more or fewer blankets in his bed, dietary supplements that may help his joints or vision or mental acuity, and attention to his physical limits (less playtime, shorter walks, etc.).

SAYING GOODBYE

One of the tragedies of loving a dog is that they often die before we do. We want them to live forever, and they want to be with us forever, but this just can't be. And like any death, no matter how prepared for it you think you may be, each is unique, and each is painful.

Fortunately, we can choose a painless and dignified death for our companion animals, and it's our obligation to do so. If your Dachshund is suffering and you can sense that it is time, you need to pay attention to the situation and do

Your friend deserves the best care you can give him until the very end.

what's best for your friend. Hopefully you won't need to make this decision in an emergency situation, but instead can take a few days or maybe weeks to spend the most quality time possible with him toward the end.

You may want to visit your veterinarian and go over your dog's symptoms and your suspicions. Especially if he's cared for your dog for a long time, your veterinarian will also care deeply about doing what's best. Ultimately, however, the decision needs to be yours and your family's.

If you have the extra time, be grateful and make as many preparations as possible so you won't need to make quick decisions you might later regret when you're overwhelmed with grief. You want to consider whether you'd prefer to have the shot administered at the veterinarian's or at your home; not all vets make house calls to do this, but some do. It's worth finding out!

Another thing to consider is what you want to do with your dog's body when he's gone. You have several options, including cremation. Many animal owners keep their pet's ashes in a special container with a photo or poem beside it. Some can bury their friend on their property, though some local laws may prohibit that. You may simply want your veterinarian to dispose of it. Be sure it's what you want.

When it's really time, however difficult it may be, try to be calm for your friend. Remember, he has spent his life being sensitive to your feelings; he will certainly know that you are very upset and that it's because of him. You want him to feel your love, not your angst. Surround him with his favorite things—a favorite toy, his softest blanket—and let everyone in the family say goodbye, including other animal friends. In the car or at home, play some relaxing music to help everyone feel more peaceful. You may want to light a candle with a favorite scent. Don't put this too close to your dog, though, as the smell may irritate him and you certainly don't want to risk dripping hot wax on him. Keep the lights low. Anyone who doesn't feel well prefers dim lighting. Sing to your friend if you want to.

Your veterinarian should explain the procedure for giving the shot and how your dog will react. If you don't understand, ask him or her to repeat it. Stay with your friend if at all possible—he needs you to help him to the other side with love. Whisper in his ear, remind him of your favorite times together, and hold him close but not too tightly. Let him know how much you love him.

When he's gone, spend as much additional time with his body as you want. After you've taken care of your dog, take care of yourself. Many people say losing a canine companion is even worse than losing a person. Dogs understand us intimately and love us unconditionally. Their loss is life-changing. Allow yourself to grieve for as long as it takes. Allow your family to grieve, and notice how the loss of your dog affects the other animals in your household.

Reflect on what was hopefully a long and full life you shared with your dog, and look forward to the time when you'll be reunited.

THE AMERICAN KENNEL CLUB BREED STANDARD

General Appearance

Low to ground, long in body and short of leg with robust muscular development, the skin is elastic and pliable without excessive wrinkling. Appearing neither crippled, awkward, nor cramped in his capacity for movement, the Dachshund is well-balanced with bold and confident head carriage and intelligent, alert facial expression. His hunting spirit, good nose, loud tongue and distinctive build make him well-suited for below-ground work and for beating the bush. His keen nose gives him an advantage over most other breeds for trailing. Note: Inasmuch as the Dachshund is a hunting dog, scars from honorable wounds shall not be considered a fault.

Size, Proportion, Substance

Bred and shown in two sizes, standard and miniature, miniatures are not a separate classification but compete in a class division for "11 pounds and under at 12 months of age and older." Weight of the standard size is usually between 16 and 32 pounds.

Head

Viewed from above or from the side, the head tapers uniformly to the tip of the nose. The eyes are of medium size, almond-shaped and dark-rimmed, with an energetic, pleasant expression; not piercing; very dark in color. The bridge bones over the eyes are strongly prominent. Wall eyes, except in the case of dappled dogs, are a serious fault. The ears are set near the top of the head, not too far forward, of moderate length, rounded, not narrow, pointed, or folded. Their carriage, when animated, is with the forward edge just touching the cheek so that the ears frame the face. The skull is slightly arched, neither too broad nor too narrow, and slopes gradually with little perceptible stop into the finely-formed, slightly arched muzzle. Black is the preferred color of the nose. Lips are tightly stretched, well covering the lower jaw. Nostrils well open. Jaws opening wide and hinged well back of the eyes, with strongly developed bones and teeth. Teeth—Powerful canine teeth; teeth fit closely together in a scissors bite. An even bite is a minor fault. Any other deviation is a serious fault.

Neck

Long, muscular, clean-cut, without dewlap, slightly arched in the nape, flowing gracefully into the shoulders.

Trunk

The trunk is long and fully muscled. When viewed in profile, the back lies in the straightest possible line between the withers and the short very slightly arched loin. A body that hangs loosely between the shoulders is a serious fault. Abdomen—Slightly drawn up.

Forequarters

For effective underground work, the front must be strong, deep, long and cleanly muscled. Forequarters in detail: Chest—The breastbone is strongly prominent in front so that on either side a depression or dimple appears. When viewed from the front, the thorax appears oval and extends downward to the mid-point of the forearm. The enclosing structure of well-sprung ribs appears full and oval to allow, by its ample capacity, complete development of heart and lungs. The keel merges gradually into the line of the abdomen and extends well beyond the front legs. Viewed in profile, the lowest point of the breast line is covered by the front leg. Shoulder Blades— Long, broad, well-laid back and firmly placed upon the fully developed thorax, closely fitted at the withers, furnished with hard yet pliable muscles. Upper Arm—Ideally the same length as the shoulder blade and at right angles to the latter, strong of bone and hard of muscle, lying close to the ribs, with elbows close to the body, yet capable of free movement. Forearm—Short; supplied with hard yet pliable muscles on the front and outside, with tightly stretched tendons on the inside and at the back, slightly curved inwards. The joints between the forearms and the feet (wrists) are closer together than the shoulder joints, so that the front does not appear absolutely straight. Knuckling over is a disqualifying fault. Feet—Front paws are full, tight, compact, with well-arched toes and tough, thick pads. They may be equally inclined a trifle outward. There are five toes, four in use, close together with a pronounced arch and strong, short nails. Front dewclaws may be removed.

Hindquarters

Strong and cleanly muscled. The pelvis, the thigh, the second thigh, and the metatarsus are ideally the same length and form a series of right angles. From the rear, the thighs are strong and powerful. The legs turn neither in nor out. Metatarsus—Short and strong, perpendicular to the second thigh bone. When viewed from behind, they are upright and parallel. Feet—Hind Paws—Smaller than the front paws with four compactly closed and arched toes with tough, thick pads. The entire foot points straight ahead and is balanced equally on the ball and not merely on the toes. Rear dewclaws should be removed. Croup—Long, rounded and full, sinking slightly toward the tail. Tail—Set in continuation of the spine, extending without kinks, twists, or pronounced curvature, and not carried too gaily.

Gait

Fluid and smooth. Forelegs reach well forward, without much lift, in unison with the driving action of hind legs. The correct shoulder assembly and well-fitted elbows allow the long, free stride in front. Viewed from the front, the legs do not move in exact parallel planes, but incline slightly inward to compensate for shortness of leg and width of chest. Hind legs drive on a line with the forelegs, with hocks (metatarsus) turning neither in nor out. The propulsion of the hind leg depends on the dog's ability to carry the hind leg to complete extension. Viewed in profile, the forward reach of the hind leg equals the rear extension. The thrust of correct movement is seen when the rear pads are clearly exposed during rear extension. Feet must travel parallel to the line of motion with no tendency to swing out, cross over, or interfere with each other. Short, choppy movement, rolling or high-stepping gait, close or overly wide coming or going are incorrect. The Dachshund must have agility, freedom of movement, and endurance to do the work for which he was developed.

Temperament

The Dachshund is clever, lively and courageous to the point of rashness, persevering in above and below ground work, with all the senses well-developed. Any display of shyness is a serious fault.

Special Characteristics of the Three Coat Varieties

The Dachshund is bred with three varieties of coat: (1) Smooth; (2) Wirehaired; (3) Longhaired and is shown in two sizes, standard and miniature. All three varieties and both sizes must conform to the characteristics already specified. The following features are applicable for each variety:

Smooth Dachshund

Coat—Short, smooth and shining. Should be neither too long nor too thick. Ears not leathery. Tail—Gradually tapered to a point, well but not too richly haired. Long sleek bristles on the underside are considered a patch of strong-growing hair, not a fault. A brush tail is a fault, as is also a partly or wholly hairless tail.

Color of Hair—Although base color is immaterial, certain patterns and basic colors predominate. One-colored Dachshunds include red (with or without a shading of interspersed dark hairs or sable) and cream. A small amount of white on the chest is acceptable, but not desirable. Nose and nails—black.

Two-colored Dachshunds include black, chocolate, wild boar, gray (blue) and fawn (Isabella), each with tan markings over the eyes, on the sides of the jaw and underlip, on the inner edge of the ear, front, breast, inside and behind the front legs, on the paws and around the anus, and from there to about one-third to one-half of the length of the tail on the underside. Undue prominence or extreme lightness of tan markings is undesirable. A small amount of white on the chest is acceptable but not desirable. Nose and nails—in the case of black dogs, black; for chocolate and all other colors, dark brown, but self-colored is acceptable.

Dappled Dachshunds—The "single" dapple pattern is expressed as lighter-colored areas contrasting with the darker base color, which may be any acceptable color. Neither the light nor the dark color should predominate. Nose and nails are the same as for one and two-colored Dachshunds. Partial or wholly blue (wall) eyes are as acceptable as dark eyes. A large area of white on the chest of a dapple is permissible.

A "double" dapple is one in which varying amounts of white coloring occur over the body in addition to the dapple pattern. Nose and nails: as for one and two-color Dachshunds; partial or wholly self-colored is permissible.

Brindle is a pattern (as opposed to a color) in which black or dark stripes occur over the entire body although in some specimens the pattern may be visible only in the tan points.

Wirehaired Dachshund

Coat—With the exception of jaw, eyebrows, and ears, the whole body is covered with a uniform tight, short, thick, rough, hard, outer coat but with finer, somewhat softer, shorter hairs (undercoat) everywhere distributed between the coarser hairs. The absence of an undercoat is a fault. The distinctive facial furnishings include a beard and eyebrows. On the ears the hair is shorter than on the body, almost smooth. The general arrangement of the hair is such that the wirehaired Dachshund, when viewed from a distance, resembles the smooth. Any sort of soft hair in the outercoat, wherever found on the body, especially on the top of the head, is a fault. The same is true of long, curly, or wavy hair, or hair that sticks out irregularly in all directions. Tail—Robust, thickly haired, gradually tapering to a point. A flag tail is a fault. Color of Hair—While the most common colors are wild boar, black and tan, and various shades of red, all colors are admissible. A small amount of white on the chest, although acceptable, is not desirable. Nose and nails—same as for the smooth variety.

Longhaired Dachshund

Coat—The sleek, glistening, often slightly wavy hair is longer under the neck and on the forechest, the underside of the body, the ears, and behind the legs. The coat gives the dog an elegant appearance. Short hair on the ear is not desirable. Too profuse a coat which masks type, equally long hair over the whole body, a curly coat, or a pronounced parting on the back are faults. Tail—Carried gracefully in prolongation of the spine; the hair attains its greatest length here and forms a veritable flag. Color of Hair—Same as for the smooth Dachshund. Nose and nails—same as for the smooth.

The foregoing description is that of the ideal Dachshund. Any deviation from the above described dog must be penalized to the extent of the deviation keeping in mind the importance of the contribution of the various features toward the basic original purpose of the breed.

Disqualification

Knuckling over of front legs

Approved April 7, 1992
Effective May 27, 1992

THE KENNEL CLUB BREED STANDARD

To read the miniature Long Haired, miniature Smooth Haired, and miniature Wire Haired standards, please refer to the Kennel Club's website at www.the-kennel-club.org.uk.

DACHSHUND (LONG HAIRED)

General Appearance

Long and low, but with compact, well muscled body, bold, defiant carriage of head and intelligent expression.

Characteristics

Intelligent, lively, courageous to the point of rashness, obedient. Especially suited to going to ground because of low build, very strong forequarters and forelegs. Long, strong jaw, and immense power of bite and hold. Excellent nose, persevering hunter and tracker.

Temperament

Faithful, versatile and good tempered.

Head and Skull

Long, appearing conical when seen from above; from side tapering uniformly to tip of nose. Skull only slightly arched. Neither too broad nor too narrow, sloping gradually without prominent stop into slightly arched muzzle. Length from tip of nose to eyes equal to length from eyes to occiput. In Wire haired, particularly, ridges over eyes strongly prominent, giving appearance of slightly broader skull. Lips well stretched, neatly covering lower jaw.

Strong jaw bones not too square or snipy, but opening wide.

Eyes
Medium size, almond-shaped, set obliquely. Dark except in chocolates, where they can be lighter. In dapples one or both 'wall' eyes permissible.

Ears
Set high, and not too far forward. Broad, of moderate length, and well rounded (not pointed or folded). Forward edge touching cheek. Mobile, and when at attention back of ear directed forward and outward.

Mouth
Teeth strongly developed, powerful canine teeth fitting closely. Jaws strong, with a perfect, regular and complete scissor bite, i.e. upper teeth closely overlapping lower teeth and set square to the jaws. Complete dentition important.

Neck
Long, muscular, clean with no dewlap, slightly arched, running in graceful lines into shoulders, carried proudly forward.

Forequarters
Shoulder blades long, broad, and placed firmly and obliquely (45 degrees to the horizontal) upon very robust rib cage. Upper arm the same length as shoulder blade, set at 90 degrees to it, very strong, and covered with hard, supple muscles. Upper arm lies close to ribs, but able to move freely. Forearm short and strong in bone, inclining slightly inwards; when seen in profile moderately straight, must not bend forward or knuckle over, which indicates unsoundness. Correctly placed foreleg should cover the lowest point of the keel.

Body
Long and full muscled. Back level, with sloping shoulders, lying in straightest possible line between withers and slightly arched loin. Loin short and strong. Breast bone strong, and so prominent that a depression appears on either side of it in front. When viewed from front, thorax full and oval; when viewed from side or above, full volumed, so allowing by its ample capacity complete development of heart and lungs. Well ribbed up, underline gradually merging into line of abdomen. Body sufficiently clear of ground to allow free movement.

Hindquarters
Rump full, broad and strong, pliant muscles. Croup long, full, robustly muscled, only slightly sloping towards tail. Pelvis strong, set obliquely and not too short. Upper thigh set at right angles to pelvis, strong and of good length. Lower thigh short, set at right angles to upper thigh and well muscled. Legs when seen behind set well apart, straight, and parallel. Hind dewclaws undesirable.

Feet
Front feet full, broad, deep, close knit, straight or very slightly turned out. Hindfeet smaller and narrower. Toes close together, with a decided arch to each toe, strong regularly placed nails, thick and firm pads. Dog must stand true, i.e. equally on all parts of the foot.

Tail
Continues line of spine, but slightly curved, without kinks or twists, not carried too high, or touching ground when at rest.

Gait/Movement
Should be free and flowing. Stride should be long, with the drive coming from the hindquarters when viewed from the side. Viewed from in front or behind, the legs and feet should move parallel to each other with the distance apart being the width of the shoulder and hip joints respectively.

Coat
Smooth-Haired: Dense, short and smooth. Hair on underside of tail coarse in texture. Skin loose and supple, but fitting closely all over without dewlap and little or no wrinkle.

Long-Haired: Soft and straight, or only slightly waved; longest under neck, on underparts of body, and behind legs, where it forms abundant feathering, on tail where it forms a flag. Outside of ears well feathered. Coat flat, and not obscuring outline. Too much hair on feet undesirable.

Wire-Haired: With exception of jaw, eyebrows, chin and ears, the whole body should be covered with a short, straight, harsh coat with dense undercoat, beard on the chin, eyebrows bushy, but hair on ears almost smooth. Legs and feet well but neatly furnished with harsh coat.

Colour

All colours allowed but (except in dapples which should be evenly marked all over) no white permissible, save for a small patch on chest which is permitted but not desirable. Nose and nails black in all colours except chocolate/tan and chocolate/dapple, where brown permitted.

Size

Ideal weight: 9-12 kgs (20-26 lbs). Miniatures Ideal weight: 4.5 kgs (10 lbs). It is of the utmost importance that judges should not award prizes to animals over 5.0 kgs (11 lbs).

Faults

Any departure from the foregoing points should be considered a fault and the seriousness with which the fault should be regarded should be in exact proportion to its degree and its effect upon the health and welfare of the dog.

Note

Male animals should have two apparently normal testicles fully descended into the scrotum.

March 1994

DACHSHUND (SMOOTH HAIRED)

General Appearance

Long and low, but with compact, well muscled body, bold, defiant carriage of head and intelligent expression.
Characteristics
Intelligent, lively, courageous to the point of rashness, obedient. Especially suited to going to ground because of low build, very strong forequarters and forelegs. Long, strong jaw, and immense power of bite and hold. Excellent nose, persevering hunter and tracker.

Temperament

Faithful, versatile and good tempered.

Head and Skull

Long, appearing conical when seen from above; from side tapering uniformly to tip of nose. Skull only slightly arched. Neither too broad nor too narrow, sloping gradually without prominent stop into slightly arched muzzle. Length from tip of nose to eyes equal to length from eyes to occiput. In Wire haired, particularly, ridges over eyes strongly prominent, giving appearance of slightly broader skull. Lips well stretched, neatly covering lower jaw. Strong jaw bones not too square or snipy, but opening wide.

Eyes

Medium size, almond-shaped, set obliquely. Dark except in chocolates, where they can be lighter. In dapples one or both 'wall' eyes permissible.

Ears

Set high, and not too far forward. Broad, of moderate length, and well rounded (not pointed or folded). Forward edge touching cheek. Mobile, and when at attention back of ear directed forward and outward.

Mouth

Teeth strongly developed, powerful canine teeth fitting closely. Jaws strong, with a perfect, regular and complete scissor bite, i.e. upper teeth closely overlapping lower teeth and set square to the jaws. Complete dentition important.

Neck

Long, muscular, clean with no dewlap, slightly arched, running in graceful lines into shoulders, carried proudly forward.

Forequarters

Shoulder blades long, broad, and placed firmly and obliquely (45 degrees to the horizontal) upon very robust rib cage. Upper arm the same length as shoulder blade, set at 90 degrees to it, very strong, and covered with hard, supple muscles. Upper arm lies close to ribs, but able to move freely. Forearm short and strong in bone, inclining slightly inwards; when seen in profile moderately straight, must not bend forward or knuckle over, which indicates unsoundness. Correctly placed foreleg should cover the lowest point of the keel.

Body

Long and full muscled. Back level, with sloping shoulders, lying in straightest possible line between withers and slightly arched loin. Loin short and strong. Breast bone strong, and so prominent that a depression appears on either side of it in front. When viewed from front, thorax full and oval; when viewed from side or above, full volumed, so allowing by its ample capacity complete development of heart and lungs. Well ribbed up, underline gradually merging into line of abdomen. Body sufficiently clear of ground to allow free movement.

Hindquarters

Rump full, broad and strong, pliant muscles. Croup long, full, robustly muscled, only slightly sloping towards tail. Pelvis strong, set obliquely and not too short. Upper thigh set at right angles to pelvis, strong and of good length. Lower thigh short, set at right angles to upper thigh and well muscled. Legs when seen behind set well apart, straight, and parallel. Hind dewclaws undesirable.

Feet

Front feet full, broad, deep, close knit, straight or very slightly turned out. Hindfeet smaller and narrower. Toes close together, with a decided arch to each toe, strong regularly placed nails, thick and firm pads. Dog must stand true, i.e. equally on all parts of the foot.

Tail

Continues line of spine, but slightly curved, without kinks or twists, not carried too high, or touching ground when at rest.

Gait/Movement

Should be free and flowing. Stride should be long, with the drive coming from the hindquarters when viewed from the side. Viewed from in front or behind, the legs and feet should move parallel to each other with the distance apart being the width of the shoulder and hip joints respectively.

Coat

Smooth-Haired: Dense, short and smooth. Hair on underside of tail coarse in texture. Skin loose and supple, but fitting closely all over without dewlap and little or no wrinkle.

Long-Haired: Soft and straight, or only slightly waved; longest under neck, on underparts of body, and behind legs, where it forms abundant feathering, on tail where it forms a flag. Outside of ears well feathered. Coat flat, and not obscuring outline. Too much hair on feet undesirable.

Wire-Haired: With exception of jaw, eyebrows, chin and ears, the whole body should be covered with a short, straight, harsh coat with dense undercoat, beard on the chin, eyebrows bushy, but hair on ears almost smooth. Legs and feet well but neatly furnished with harsh coat.

Colour

All colours allowed but (except in dapples which should be evenly marked all over) no white permissible, save for a small patch on chest which is permitted but not desirable. Nose and nails black in all colours except chocolate/tan and chocolate/dapple, where brown permitted.

Size

Ideal weight: 9-12 kgs (20-26 lbs). Miniatures Ideal weight: 4.5 kgs (10 lbs). It is of the utmost importance that judges should not award prizes to animals over 5.0 kgs (11 lbs).

Faults

Any departure from the foregoing points should be considered a fault and the seriousness with which the fault should be regarded should be in exact proportion to its degree and its effect upon the health and welfare of the dog.

Note

Male animals should have two apparently normal testicles fully descended into the scrotum.

March 1994

DACHSHUND (WIRE HAIRED)

General Appearance

Long and low, but with compact, well muscled body, bold, defiant carriage of head and intelligent expression.

Characteristics

Intelligent, lively, courageous to the point of rashness, obedient. Especially suited to going to ground because of low build, very strong forequarters and forelegs. Long, strong jaw, and immense power of bite and hold. Excellent nose, persevering hunter and tracker.

Temperament

Faithful, versatile and good tempered.

Head and Skull

Long, appearing conical when seen from above; from side tapering uniformly to tip of nose. Skull only slightly arched. Neither too broad nor too narrow, sloping gradually without prominent stop into slightly arched muzzle. Length from tip of nose to eyes equal to length from eyes to occiput. In Wire haired, particularly, ridges over eyes strongly prominent, giving appearance of slightly broader skull. Lips well stretched, neatly covering lower jaw. Strong jaw bones not too square or snipy, but opening wide.

Eyes

Medium size, almond-shaped, set obliquely. Dark except in chocolates, where they can be lighter. In dapples one or both 'wall' eyes permissible.

Ears

Set high, and not too far forward. Broad, of moderate length, and well rounded (not pointed or folded). Forward edge touching cheek. Mobile, and when at attention back of ear directed forward and outward.

Mouth

Teeth strongly developed, powerful canine teeth fitting closely. Jaws strong, with a perfect, regular and complete scissor bite, i.e. upper teeth closely overlapping lower teeth and set square to the jaws. Complete dentition important.

Neck

Long, muscular, clean with no dewlap, slightly arched, running in graceful lines into shoulders, carried proudly forward.

Forequarters

Shoulder blades long, broad, and placed firmly and obliquely (45 degrees to the horizontal) upon very robust rib cage. Upper arm the same length as shoulder blade, set at 90 degrees to it, very strong, and covered with hard, supple muscles. Upper arm lies close to ribs, but able to move freely. Forearm short and strong in bone, inclining slightly inwards; when seen in profile moderately straight, must not bend forward or knuckle over, which indicates unsoundness. Correctly placed foreleg should cover the lowest point of the keel.

Body

Long and full muscled. Back level, with sloping shoulders, lying in straightest possible line between withers and slightly arched loin. Loin short and strong. Breast bone strong, and so prominent that a depression appears on either side of it in front. When viewed from front, thorax full and oval; when viewed from side or above, full volumed, so allowing by its ample capacity complete development of heart and lungs. Well ribbed up, underline gradually merging into line of abdomen. Body sufficiently clear of ground to allow free movement.

Hindquarters

Rump full, broad and strong, pliant muscles. Croup long, full, robustly muscled, only slightly sloping towards tail. Pelvis strong, set obliquely and not too short. Upper thigh set at right angles to pelvis, strong and of good length. Lower thigh short, set at right angles to upper thigh and well muscled. Legs when seen behind set well apart, straight, and parallel. Hind dewclaws undesirable.

Feet

Front feet full, broad, deep, close knit, straight or very slightly turned out. Hindfeet smaller and narrower. Toes close together, with a decided arch to each toe, strong regularly placed nails, thick and firm pads. Dog must stand true, i.e. equally on all parts of the foot.

Tail

Continues line of spine, but slightly curved, without kinks or twists, not carried too high, or touching ground when at rest.

Gait/Movement

Should be free and flowing. Stride should be long, with the drive coming from the hindquarters when viewed from the side. Viewed from in front or behind, the legs and feet should move parallel to each other with the distance apart being the width of the shoulder and hip joints respectively.

Coat

Smooth-Haired: Dense, short and smooth. Hair on underside of tail coarse in texture. Skin loose and supple, but fitting closely all over without dewlap and little or no wrinkle.

Long-Haired: Soft and straight, or only slightly waved; longest under neck, on underparts of body, and behind legs, where it forms abundant feathering, on tail where it forms a flag. Outside of ears well feathered. Coat flat, and not obscuring outline. Too much hair on feet undesirable.

Wire-Haired: With exception of jaw, eyebrows, chin and ears, the whole body should be covered with a short, straight, harsh coat with dense undercoat, beard on the chin, eyebrows bushy, but hair on ears almost smooth. Legs and feet well but neatly furnished with harsh coat.

Colour

All colours allowed but (except in dapples which should be evenly marked all over) no white permissible, save for a small patch on chest which is permitted but not desirable. Nose and nails black in all colours except chocolate/tan and chocolate/dapple, where brown permitted.

Size

Ideal weight: 9-12 kgs (20-26 lbs). Miniatures Ideal weight: 4.5 kgs (10 lbs). It is of the utmost importance that judges should not award prizes to animals over 5.0 kgs (11 lbs).

Faults

Any departure from the foregoing points should be considered a fault and the seriousness with which the fault should be regarded should be in exact proportion to its degree and its effect upon the health and welfare of the dog.

Note

Male animals should have two apparently normal testicles fully descended into the scrotum.

March 1994

CONVERSION CHART

US UNITS	MULTIPLIED BY	EQUALS METRIC UNITS
Length		
Inches	2.5400	Centimeters
Feet	0.3048	Meters
Yards	0.9144	Meters
Miles	1.6093	Kilometers
Area		
Square inches	6.4516	Square centimeters
Square feet	0.0929	Square meters
Square yards	0.8361	Square meters
Acres	0.4047	Hectares
Volume		
Cubic feet	0.0283	Cubic meters
Cubic yards	0.7646	Cubic meters
Gallons	3.7854	Liters
Weight		
Foot-pounds	1.3830	Newton-meters
Pounds	0.4536	Kilograms

Temperature

Fahrenheit to Celsius: Subtract 32 from the Fahrenheit temperature.
Divide the answer by 9, then multiply by 5.

Organizations

American Boarding Kennels Association
4575 Galley Road
Suite 400A
Colorado Springs, CO 80915
E-mail: info@abka.com
www.abka.com

American Kennel Club (AKC)
5580 Centerview Drive
Raleigh, NC 27606
Telephone: (919) 233-9767
Fax: (919) 233-3627
E-mail: info@akc.org
www.akc.org

Association for Pet Loss and Bereavement, Inc. (APLB)
P.O. Box 106
Brooklyn, NY 11230
(718) 382-0690
E-mail: aplb@aplb.org
www.aplb.org

Association of Pet Dog Trainers (APDT)
150 Executive Center Drive Box 35
Greenville, SC 29615
Telephone: (800) PET-DOGS
Fax: (864) 331-0767
www.apdt.com

Canadian Kennel Club (CKC)
89 Skyway Avenue, Suite 100
Etobicoke, Ontario M9W 6R4
Telephone: (416) 675-5511
Fax: (416) 675-6506
E-mail: information@ckc.ca
www.ckc.ca

Delta Society
875 124th Ave NE, suite 101
Bellevue, WA 98005
Telephone: (425) 226-7357
Fax: (425) 235-1076
E-mail: info@deltasociety.org
www.deltasociety.org

The Dachshund Club (UK)
Secretary: Mrs. A. Moore
E-mail: secretary@dachshund-club.co.uk
www.dachshundclub.co.uk

The Dachshund Club of America
Secretary: Andra H. O'Connell
www.dachshund-dca.org

The Kennel Club (UK)
1 Clarges Street
London
W1J 8AB
Telephone: 0870 606 6750
Fax: 0207 518 1058
www.the-kennel-club.org.uk

National Dog Groomers Association of America
P.O. Box 101
Clark, PA 16113
(724) 962-2711
E-mail: ndga@nationaldog-groomers.com
www.nationaldoggroomers.com

North American Dog Agility Council
11522 South Hwy 3
Cataldo, ID 83810
E-mail: info@nadac.com
www.nadac.com

Therapy Dogs International
88 Bartley Road
Flanders, New Jersey 07836
(973) 252-9800
E-mail: tdi@gti.net
www.tdi-dog.org

United Kennel Club (UKC)
100 E. Kilgore Road
Kalamazoo, MI 49002-5584
Telephone: (269) 343-9020
Fax: (269) 343-7037
E-mail: pbickell@ukcdogs.com
www.ukcdogs.com

United States Dog Agility Association, Inc. (USDAA)
P.O. Box 850955
Richardson, TX 75085-0955
Telephone: (972) 487-2200
Fax: (972) 272-4404
E-mail: info@usdaa.com
www.usdaa.com

Veterinary Pet Insurance
P.O. Box 2344
Brea, CA 92822-2344
Telephone: (800) USA-PETS
www.petinsurance.com

Magazines

AKC Family Dog
American Kennel Club
260 Madison Avenue
New York, NY 10016
Telephone: (800) 490-5675
E-mail: familydog@akc.org
www.akc.org/pubs/familydog

AKC Gazette
American Kennel Club
260 Madison Avenue
New York, NY 10016
Telephone: (800) 533-7323
E-mail: gazette@akc.org
www.akc.org/pubs/gazette

The Bark
2810 8th St.
Berkeley, CA 94710
Telephone: (877) BARKNEWS
Fax: (510) 704-0933
E-mail: customerservice@the-bark.com
www.thebark.com

Dog & Kennel
Pet Publishing, Inc.
7-L Dundas Circle
Greensboro, NC 27407
Telephone: (336) 292-4272
Fax: (336) 292-4272
E-mail: info@petpublishing.com
www.dogandkennel.com

Dog Fancy
Subscription Department
P.O. Box 53264
Boulder, CO 80322-3264
Telephone: (800) 365-4421
E-mail: barkback@dogfancy.com
www.dogfancy.com

Dogs Monthly
Ascot House
High Street, Ascot,
Berkshire SL5 7JG
United Kingdom
Telephone: 0870 730 8433
Fax: 0870 730 8431
E-mail: admin@rtc-associates.freeserve.co.uk
www.corsini.co.uk/dogsmonthly

Reading

Anderson, Teoti. *The Super Simple Guide to Housetraining.* TFH Publications, Inc. 2004.

Bauer, Nona Kilgore. *Adopting a Great Dog.* TFH Publications, Inc. 2003.

Beauchamp, Richard. *The Simple Guide to Showing Your Dog*. TFH Publications, Inc. 2003.

Billinghurst, Dr. Ian. *Give Your Dog a Bone*. Ian Billinghurst, 1993.

Giffin, James M., MD, and Lisa Carlson, DVM. *Dog Owner's Home Veterinary*

Handbook, 3rd Edition. Howell Book House 1999.

King, Trish. *Parenting Your Dog*. TFH Publications, Inc. 2004.

MacDonald, Carina Beth. *Raw Dog Food: Make It Easy for You and Your Dog*. Dogwise Publishing, 2003.

Morgan, Diane. *Good Dogkeeping: Today's Guide for Caring for Your Best Friend*. TFH Publications, Inc. 2004.

Morgan, Diane. *The Simple Guide to Grooming Your Dog*. TFH Publications, Inc. 2003.

Nock, Anne. *A Boston's World*. Pickmick Publishing Company 1998.

Philbin, Tom. *The Simple Guide to Dog Training*. TFH Publications, Inc. 2002.

Wood, Deborah. *Little Dogs: Training Your Pint-Sized Canine Companion*. TFH Publications, Inc. 2004.

Yin, Sophia, DVM. *How to Behave so Your Dog Behaves*. TFH Publications, Inc. 2004.

Useful Websites

For those who can't get enough Dachshund, check out these websites. They offer everything from care tips to chat groups to photo contests—anything and everything Dachshund owners care about.
www.thedachshundnetwork.com
www.dachshundsatoz.net
www.doxiedelight.com
www.dachshund-dogs.com

Animal Welfare Groups and Rescue Organizations

American Humane Association (AHA)
63 Inverness Drive East
Englewood, CO 80112
Telephone: (303) 792-9900
Fax: 792-5333
www.americanhumane.org

American Society for the Prevention of Cruelty to Animals (ASPCA)
424 E. 92nd Street
New York, NY 10128-6804
Telephone: (212) 876-7700
www.aspca.org

Royal Society for the Prevention of Cruelty to Animals (RSPCA)
Telephone: 0870 3335 999
Fax: 0870 7530 284
www.rspca.org.uk
The Humane Society of the United States (HSUS)
2100 L Street, NW
Washington DC 20037
Telephone: (202) 452-1100
www.hsus.org

Veterinary Resources

American Academy of Veterinary Acupuncture (AAVA)
66 Morris Avenue, Suite 2A
Springfield, NJ 07081
Telephone: (973) 379-1100
E-mail: office@aava.org
www.aava.org

American Animal Hospital Association (AAHA)
P.O. Box 150899
Denver, CO 80215-0899
Telephone: (303) 986-2800
Fax: (303) 986-1700
E-mail: info@aahanet.org
www.aahanet.org

American College of Veterinary Ophthalmologists (ACVO)
P.O. Box 1311
Mediridan, Idaho 83680
Telephone: (208) 466-7624
E-mail: office@acvo.org
www.acvo.com

American Veterinary Chiropractic Association (AVCA)
442154 E 140 Road
Bluejacket, OK 74333
Telephone: (918) 784-2231
E-mail: amvetchiro@aol.com
www.animalchiropractic.org

American Veterinary Medical Association (AVMA)
1931 North Meacham Road, Suite 100
Schaumburg, IL 60173
Telephone: (847) 925-8070
Fax: (847) 925-1329
E-mail: avmainfo@avma.org
www.avma.org

British Veterinary Association (BVA)
7 Mansfield Street
London, England
W1G 9NQ
Telephone: 020 7636 6541
Fax: 020 7436 2970
E-mail: bvahq@bva.co.uk
www.bva.co.uk

International Veterinary Acupuncture Society (IVAS)
P.O. Box 271395
Fort Collins, CO 80527
Telephone: (970) 266-0666
Fax: (970) 260-0777
E-mail: office@ivas.org
www.ivas.org

Emergency Phone Numbers

ASPCA Animal Poison Control Center
(888) 426-4435
A $50 consultation fee may be applied to your credit card.
National Dog Registry (NDR)
Telephone: (800) 637-3647
E-mail: info@natldogregistry.com
www.natldogregistry.com

DEDICATION

For my family, and for Nikole Knobloch

PHOTO CREDITS

Photo on pages 47, 61, 67, 79, 80, 81, and 104 courtesy of Kathy Bontz

Photo on front cover and photos on pages 18, 74, 75, 83, and 99 courtesy of Paulette Braun

All other photos courtesy of Isabelle Francais